ERIC HURLM

SURVIVING OURSELVES

The Evolution of Community,
Education, and Agriculture
in the 21st Century

**dreamriver
press**

Dreamriver Press LLC
www.dreamriverpress.com
and at:
19 Grace Court, Apt. 2D
Brooklyn, NY 11201
U.S.A.

First Dreamriver Press edition, 2012

ISBN-13: 978-0-9831315-1-9
ISBN-10: 0-9831315-1-1

Library of Congress Control Number: 2010928701

1. NAT011000-NATURE / Environmental Conservation & Protection
2. NAT038000-NATURE / Natural Resources
3. SOC055000-SOCIAL SCIENCE / Agriculture and Food

Designed by George D. Matthiopoulos

Printed on 100% recycled paper

Printed and bound in Canada

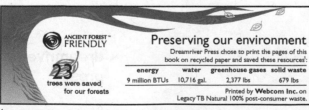

ANCIENT FOREST™
FRIENDLY

23
trees were saved
for our forests

Preserving our environment
Dreamriver Press chose to print the pages of this
book on recycled paper and saved these resources[1]:

	energy	water	greenhouse gases	solid waste
	9 million BTUs	10,716 gal.	2,377 lbs	679 lbs

Printed by **Webcom Inc.** on
Legacy TB Natural 100% post-consumer waste.

[1]Estimates were made using the Environmental Defense Paper Calculator.

99 %

FSC
www.fsc.org

MIX
Paper from
responsible sources
FSC® C004071

Dedicated to

*Waunxpewichakhiya, Tokala Wacipi,
Pejihota, and Tawaka.*

Also, to

*The **strength** that exists in all of us to survive.
The **love** that binds us all together to exist peacefully.
The **resistance** to being mindless slaves to any system.
The **clarity** to accept who we are
    and what we are intended to do.*

I don't know how to save the world. I don't have the answers or The Answer. I hold no secret knowledge as to how to fix the mistakes of generations past and present. I only know that without compassion and respect for *all* of Earth's inhabitants, none of us will survive—nor will we deserve to.

—LEONARD PELTIER

body and mind
earth and sky

Contents

Acknowledgements

A special thanks to my two sons for choosing me as your flesh-and-bone father and helping me see life from a different perspective. May your vibrant energy, creativity, and imagination continue to flourish.

Thanks to loved ones who have supported my writings throughout the years: Ali, Beverly, Kay, Ryan, Kyle, and others. Your words of encouragement have helped me more than you will ever know.

Thanks to Mom, Dad, and Donnie for your love and guidance.

Thanks to my high school English teacher, Trecie Sides-Wallace. You always demanded my best and believed in me. I will never forget that you saw more in me than I was willing to accept at the time.

Thanks to Theodore and Maria for taking a chance on a farm boy. Your genuine kindness is an inspiration.

Thanks to all those who contributed to this book, especially the interviewees.

Thanks to all who read my words and agree.

Thanks to all who read my words and disagree.

Thanks to the words that come through me.

Foreword

"Apartheid" means separation. Eco-apartheid refers to our separation from the Earth, and this separation is at the root of our not understanding and feeling the living Earth, Her potential for providing us with abundance, and our potential to be cocreators with Her gifts of seed and soil.

Eco-apartheid allows agriculture to become a war against the Earth, Her biodiversity, and people. If we were sensitive to the living seed and living soil, we would not develop genetically engineered seeds with pesticides built into them (Bt crops) or seeds that tolerate higher doses of herbicide. We definitely would not develop terminator technology to deliberately make seeds sterile.

If we had a deep awareness of the life in the soil, we would not pour synthetic fertilizers on it, fooling ourselves into believing that we are "improving soil fertility" while we are in fact killing the source of its fertility—microorganisms—and creating sterile soil.

If we realized that we are part of the web of life, not its creators and masters, we would not allow patents on life and patents on seed, which are based on the false assumptions that life is an "invention" and that the "inventors" are its owners. We would not senselessly spray pesticides, and spread pesticide-producing GM crops, which are killing friendly insects and leading to the disappearance of bees.

Not only are other species being killed at an unprecedented rate and scale because of an agriculture that has become like war—humans, too, are being killed. A quarter million Indian farmers have been pushed to suicide in little over a decade because of a debt trap created by patented GM seeds. Most suicides are in the cotton belt, and most cotton is now Monsanto's Bt Cotton.

Industrial agriculture is promoted as a solution to hunger. But it creates hunger. It creates hunger because it produces commodities, not food. Commodities go to feed cars and factory farms, not people. That's why one billion people are hungry. And another two billion suffer from food-related diseases such as obesity and diabetes. An agriculture based on war against the Earth is a war against our bodies, because we are the Earth.

And while it creates the illusion of "more," it generates scarcity at every level. Nonrenewable seeds are creating a seed famine in India, a country where a decade ago every farmer had a diversity of renewable seeds. Chemicals are desertifying our farms and our diet. And a monocultural agriculture based on high inputs of cash, chemicals, and fossil fuels is the basis of a negative economy of debt, dispossession, waste, and pollution.

Eco-apartheid gives rise to ignorance combined with arrogance. It gives rise to recklessness and irresponsibility. It gives rise to mistaking destruction for creation, and creation for passivity. A violent mind cannot participate in the nonviolent creativity of the Earth. It can only destroy. It can only develop instruments of war.

We need a transition to nonviolence, in our minds and in our relationship with the Earth. We need to recognize that we are part of the living Earth, not Her conquerors and masters. We need to make a paradigm shift from eco-apartheid to Earth democracy—living on the Earth as a member of the Earth family.

This is the paradigm shift we started in Navdanya 25 years ago, growing more food by working with the Earth, not against Her. And this is what Eric has done. He has become the change he wants to see. And often his intimate cooperation with the soil as a farmer has grown not just healthy crops, but an ethics of an Earth community. As a farmer poet, Eric is walking in the footsteps of our dear, beloved Wendell Berry. I am sure you will be as inspired as I have been in reading the poetry of the land from the next generation.

Dr. Vandana Shiva

Power of the Storm
Accepting Our Strength

> *Every human being is a raindrop. And when enough of the raindrops*
> *become clear and coherent they then become the power of the storm.*
>
> JOHN TRUDELL

Human Spirit is an extension of Mother Nature, just as Mother Nature is an extension of Human Spirit. One mirrors the other, reflecting it in different forms. Nature reminds us of the beauty within. The Human Spirit is intended to translate Nature's expressions and intentions into song, story, photography, poetry, or a lesson learned. When the two coexist in harmony, there is no greater expression of love, freedom, beauty, power, grace, bliss, and brilliance. Only Nature and the Human Spirit in healthy balance can truly express limitless being. Both embody higher consciousness. Both are creators. Nature and the Human Spirit are constantly evolving, expanding, and intensifying in purpose. But when the two are separated or in opposition, all living things suffer physically, emotionally, and spiritually. This is when we exchange creation for destruction.

Human Spirit is our link to all living things, our cosmic connection to the rest of the universe. It is a doorway to who we really are or at least who we are intended to be. As we step across that threshold, we are slowly stepping into the magic that is ourselves. The further inside we venture, the more we discover about where we've gone, who we've been, who we are supposed to be, and what we are intended to do. We also see the significance of lessons already learned and the remaining lessons we are meant to learn. To never walk through that door is to ignore the greatest gift of existence. To disregard Nature is to sever every last thread connecting us to the universe's cosmic web.

Unexplained species die-offs such as Colony Collapse Disorder (CCD) of honeybees and White-Nose Syndrome of bats plague us. Decimation of monarch butterflies is occurring due to widespread destruction of their milkweed habitat from the excessive use of the herbicide Roundup. Many other species are being impacted by our other destructive habits. Species as small as the bumblebee and as large as the elephant have experienced a drastic decline in their numbers. Fish populations have been decimated by the excesses of commercial fishing. Between 1970 and 2005, the overall populations of land-based, marine, and freshwater species declined by 27 percent, according to the WWF's Living Planet Index. Yet, humanity's growth rate continues to accelerate. Surely, this growth cannot be sustained, as we need and depend on other species for our own survival. We are merely one thread in the web of life and can't continue to spin our own thread while destroying the others. The web of life cannot remain strong with only one species flourishing.

Halfway into 2012, widespread chaos consumes our planet—politically, socially, environmentally, and spiritually. But we're still here. Although we are encumbered, we haven't been annihilated. Occupy Wall Street has transformed into Occupy Everything. The 99 percent has become restless. It is obvious—more and more individuals are seeking a balanced existence, contrary to the corrupt systems that have been the status quo for way too long. It is important that we understand the significance not only of who we are, but what we are experiencing. Those who seek a balanced relationship with Nature are extremely important people. Our existence is not to be taken lightly—it is not coincidental that we are where we are at this time. All of what has happened is for a purpose. Despite the damage that has occurred up to now, everything can still be corrected, the Earth can still be healed. We can still determine the outcome. Our awareness must awaken within to inspire change in others.

This is a journey we need to embark on *now*—physically, spiritually, and emotionally. There is a need for us not only to recognize our spiritual connection to Nature, but also to allow Nature and ourselves to exist as one. We will need to accept the incredible workload ahead, while overcoming a tornado of emotional conflict. For this radical shift to take place, a serious change must occur in not only our mentality, but also in our daily actions. This evolution is not about idolatry, paganism, or worshipping a specific deity. It is founded more in humanism. It is about consciousness. It is an expression of our survival instinct. It is about living. Specifically, it is a reawakening—an awareness and acceptance of what was intended of our Earthly experience. The first step is to free our minds . . . the rest of our existence will surely follow.

Centuries of smoke screens and mirrors have left us with a society in which the Human Spirit is struggling to function properly. It is no coincidence that we've simultaneously severed our ties with Nature and created a world where everything is a commodity rather than an extension of ourselves. It is easy to lose ourselves in our lifestyles reliant on computers, satellites, touch screens, and other clever devices, but in doing so, we're merely attempting to conceal our existential inadequacies with technological ingenuity.

Minds, hearts, and bodies are out of sync with the beat of the sacred drum. Wanting to break free, we're constantly coerced back in line with more rules, laws, and codes for living. Our spirits are sacrificed daily on an altar built on the misconceptions of time, money, religion, and ego. The smoke chokes our natural existence. Deep down we know we are suffocating our inner being, the part that screams for us to be who we are meant to be. It takes true strength to overcome this suppression, and regain a connection to Nature. Those of us with this strength, with this knowledge and experience have a duty to awaken others and help guide them back to Nature.

The reality in which we currently reside is a house of cards tumbling down all around us. That karmic Milky Way where flesh falls from the bone, revealing our true being is seldom witnessed. Instead we're convincing ourselves that this stagnant pool of sterile emotion is living. Now is the time to leave that world. Now is the time to let our consciousness overcome ego and fear. Now is the time to reintroduce ourselves to who we truly are.

Our oceans provide the perfect example of the reckless behavior that must be altered. The Gulf of Mexico was flooded with oil and then toxic dispersants in 2010. The Pacific Ocean has slowly been nuked with radiation from Japan's Fukushima Daiichi nuclear power plant since April 2011, while square-mile chunks of ice from the poles are cannonballing into frigid waters. Do we ignore the impact of these events and proceed with business as usual? Or do we learn from these disasters and change horses midstream?

It is easy to say we are not the ones in charge. It is easy to say we are not the ones making the decisions that put the health of our environment and ourselves at stake. I mean, who among us has ever launched a nuclear bomb or spilled millions of gallons of oil into the ocean or flooded rivers with poisonous chemicals? It is even easy to argue that the people running governments and corporations will never read these words and wouldn't flinch an inch if they did. But we can no longer place the blame elsewhere to justify our lack of effort. We do not make the decisions for ExxonMobil or Monsanto or Coca-Cola or Peabody Energy, but we do make our own personal decisions that impact many others around us. Change begins within. These are not expected to be painless days we find ourselves living through. We can no longer afford polite questions and passive responses.

The days we are now living are very significant. We are very fortunate to be alive at this time. Why us? Why now? We are all potential warriors, healers, teachers, and leaders. Each passing moon reveals us for who we once were, who we truly are, and who we were always intended to be. Only those who have the will, the hope, the strength, the awareness, and the love will choose the correct destination at the fork in the road.

I am speaking about the survival of the Human Spirit. I am speaking about the evolution of our higher consciousness. That aspect of our being that is godly, that is very much aware of all existence, of our connection to all things. We are all creators. What we think, we create on one level or another. Our thoughts are like pebbles tossed into a cosmic pond, sending forth ripples across the universe. Our actions and reactions ride the waves from the initial splash. The bigger the pebble, the bigger the splash. We have the powerful choice of creating either more fear and destruction or more enlightenment and harmony. There are two roads diverging in a yellow wood. The choice of direction is ours—individually and collectively.

We do not need some scientist in a laboratory to come forth with the startling announcement that we are connected to others on a microscopic level through our DNA. We do not need a televangelist crying for money to convince us of the significance of our soul. We do not need a politician or an advertising jingle to sell us hope and freedom. Deep inside, we already know these truths. We only have to look within to discover the secrets of the universe.

For many generations we have lived wounded. We've been hurting, longing for sacred medicine to calm us, to quiet our fears. Yet we've resisted change because of those fears. We've not allowed our true selves to lead us through our days and nights to become the people, the warriors, the healers, the teachers, the students, the unique species we are meant to be in this world, on this Earth.

We are taught to live in fear. Taught to feel guilty if we don't live in fear. Guilt is one of humanity's cruelest tricks. It crawls up your spine, and with its steely fangs, leaves a bloody trail of metal toothprints behind before it buries itself in the back of your neck, digging for your mind and swimming for your soul. Through flesh, blood, and millions of tiny cells it finds you. It starts with the weakest parts so you don't notice the damage until your strongest traits begin to fade. By then it appears too late, but recovery is inevitable. It always takes more time than the transgression itself because it requires much more effort to overcome something once you've surrendered to its domination. Combine guilt with misconceptions about sin and blame, and you have one hell of a dark swamp to find your way out of each and every day. It's too late in the game to be pointing fingers at who caused this or allowed that. Everyone has to work together from this point forward.

How have we gotten to this point? We live in a world of diminishing resources where the rivers and oceans are polluted with our toxic lifestyles based on concrete and steel, greed and depression. Our home has become a playground where we kill as many trees and as much soil as possible simply for financial gain and the illusion of prosperity. We turn our eyes from the vibrant colors of Nature toward the glowing screens of light in our living rooms. The beating of the sacred drum is ignored as we listen to the idle conversations of talking television-heads focused on nothing but chatter and ill-founded opinions. They tell us what to think, who to vote for, who to hate, who to believe, who to fear, who to trust, what to buy, when to change our clocks, how long to sleep, what to eat, what to drive, what to drink, what is acceptable or not, where to travel, and when it is safe to come out of our homes. We must ignore these people we'll never meet and listen to our own hearts . . . not their mouths, egos, or opinions.

Their wars are waged upon emotive nouns—drugs, terror, evil, or whichever term is manufactured by the public relations people paid to brain-stain our minds with the latest, scariest boogeyman hiding in the closet or under our bed. War is often nothing more than one culture robbing another, pillaging resources for profit, and is often a cleverly disguised transfer of wealth. Who are we kidding? Warring countries are in the resource robbery business—it's not about preserving freedom. Throughout history, the agendas have been about corporate and political powers disguising themselves as Good Samaritans, when in actuality they are nothing more than wolves in sheep's clothing. They are the most powerfully persuasive salesmen feeding on two things we hold sacred—faith and loyalty. Faith to one's idea of God, and loyalty to one's idea of country.

Putting our trust in corporate, religious, and political leaders to do their jobs, we go about our daily business. Distracted, we transform ourselves into specialized members of a vast assembly line. Even if we see a problem existing elsewhere we are convinced it is not our duty to address it. But not all medical and human health problems are to be left up to doctors and nurses. Not all agriculture problems are to be left up to farmers and ranchers. Not all environmental problems are to be left up to environmental groups. Not all political problems are to be left up to politicians. Recognizing a problem and talking about a problem does not solve the problem. Neither does counting on the organizations whose purpose it is to combat key issues. It is the duty of all of us to battle as many wrongs as possible. To do this effectively we need to be vigilant, active, and use our own minds, hearts, and spirits. They are our true compass, our most reliable indicator of what we must do.

What are we really expecting to gain if we carry on with all these confusing power struggles? If we are truly honest with ourselves, it is obvious we are sacrificing far more than we could ever gain. For thousands of years in primitive cultures and tribes across the globe, a sacrifice performed as a ritual ceremony has always been meant to honor a person, a spirit, or an event. What do we honor with our sacrifice of Nature, with our sacrifice of the Human Spirit? Is it money? Comfort? Convenience? Luxury? Numbness?

These are harsh accusations, I know. I, too, feel their sting. But still, I must continue with this examination of our human motives to make sense of our actions and to see how desperately we need to change them in order to survive the difficult transition ahead.

Let us ask ourselves one question: Who is truly prospering? For after more than a century of commercialism, consumerism, and capitalism the false promises of perpetual growth and wealth are killing us slowly and methodically. As we continue to adopt more of these delusions marketed by political tricksters and corporate mind manipulators, we tighten the noose around the necks not only of ourselves, but of our children, grandchildren, and great-grandchildren.

Instead, our focus should be on the essentials of living:

1. Water
2. Food
3. Shelter
4. Nature's healing powers
5. Love and strength

Most talk shows and talking heads focus on political or religious hot-button issues that divide people according to their different beliefs. What good are political or religious beliefs without healthy food and clean water? Are we focusing on the magician's busy hand while the truly "magical hand" beneath the table steals the show? By ignoring our food and water supply, we are falling for the greatest scam any magician or illusionist can play on an audience . . . one that convinces us that everything else is more important than what we eat and drink.

As we waltz to a hypnotic beat through this world, I can't help but think back to the type of life John Lennon advocated. How he lived his life showed us what the world could and can still be if we are strong enough to stand up to our fears and the mindless money machine. Lennon once said, "Nobody controls me. I'm uncontrollable. The only one who can control me is me." No one can control us if we refuse to be controlled. Only we have the power to set ourselves free.

As "consumers" in this world, as representatives of 99 percent of the population, think of the real power we have. I believe the Occupy Wall Street movement is part of the initial stages of the general awakening transpiring throughout the world. Contemplate the raw genuine power of persuasion we have as the living and breathing souls who purchase the majority of the goods needed to make this economics-obsessed world spin round. It's easy to see we have the power. If we join together in spirit, in thought, in real persuasive power, we are truly the ones who could run the show . . . despite our peasant status. Not the royal families and billionaire tycoons who mask their prop-town existence with false power and wealth, not the corrupt politicians who disgrace the very idea of freedom, and certainly not the banks and corporations who cower behind their logos. We, the majority, are the real-life humans who make this planet spin round. We're convinced we are nothing more than necessary slaves, but it just isn't so. Without our cooperation, the "elite" would cease to be . . . well, elite. Unconsciously, we fund the greatest scam in the history of the planet . . . an economic system designed to enrich only one percent of the more than seven billion people on this planet. Rather than funding this corrupt system, why not construct our own paradigm where we can see the physical, emotional, spiritual, and financial benefits in our own lives, within our own families and communities?

When our mind, body, and spirit are able to function as one in harmony, there is no greater joy to be experienced. This joyful state is what our experience as humans is intended to be. But we have allowed a society to develop that refuses such a balance, thus denying the orchestra of our soul the chance to play with all the instruments necessary to express its full potential. But as the moons come and go, as the sun rises and sets, more and more of life is coming into such harmony, more instruments and musicians are coming on stage. Once everyone is in tune with each other, we will witness just how incredible we are meant to be.

How can we achieve this? By participating in or directly experiencing any number of actions that help us connect with Nature. Here are just a few activities that will help get us on that path or farther down along it:

1. Watch the sun rise or set whenever possible.
2. Walk barefoot on the Earth every day, whether on grass or bare earth.
3. Sit in complete silence, close your eyes, and listen to Nature as often as possible.
4. Find a favorite place in Nature to think or meditate daily (even if it's a place created in your mind).
5. Plant a garden and trees every year, no matter how small or how many.
6. Eat fresh organic fruit and vegetables every day.
7. Speak to all creatures lovingly and with respect and treat them as an extension of your own family.
8. Smile and laugh more.
9. Observe and learn from Nature's signs.
10. Give more back to Nature than you take.

Rhyme and Reason

This book before you is an exploration of the ever-present, poignant relationship between Nature and the Human Spirit. It is evident that the majority of us do not fully realize what we are doing to ourselves, our environment, and our future. It is still within us to wake up and see just how big the elephant in the room really is. Our ongoing repetition of character and behavior is baffling. I'm often amazed, even dumbfounded, at what we accept as status quo and the maddening motivations behind our methods.

By the same token, I'm fascinated with the small minority of people who dare to try to change this world for the better against the greatest of odds. In their stories, intentions, and persuasions I find strength and hope for a better existence. It is easy to be pessimistic these days . . . which is why I'm focusing chiefly on optimistic individuals and their ideas, actions, and reactions to all the madness in this modern world. The poetry in this book explores both sides of the emotional coin in our role as thinkers, observers, and doers, exploiting the dark clouds and silver linings of our thoughts and actions. It is also imperative we attempt to understand the reasons for the apathy, carelessness, and recklessness that have contributed to the overwhelming devastation of our resources, vital wildlife, and many wonders of Nature.

Whether it is through the heavily commercialized industries of agriculture, oil, coal, timber, housing, bottled water, or ornamental flowers, Nature often loses in our quest for materialistic gain. In our desecration of Nature, we've severed ties to parts of our selves. This is the real meat and potatoes of who we are or at least who we are intended to be. Awareness of this severance does not give me a sense of superiority but rather a keen sense of responsibility to speak my mind in my own words. As long as we continue to do nothing and say nothing, nothing will happen. There will be no change for the better— no miraculous transformation through the manifestation of our individual and collective genius . . . only more of the same. Change is only possible if we begin to quickly awaken to all the absurdities transpiring around us.

Through the stories of others connecting or reconnecting with Nature, the beautiful meaning of our existence is revealed. By healing and harmonizing Her, the significance of our role as humans and our sacred connection to all living things is evident. Through their examples of leadership, courage, determination, and love we see, hear, and feel what is possible. These stories find not only the dream and the dreamer, but the deed and the doer.

The vast majority of us are not climatologists, geologists, or astrologists, but we are life forms in search of the meaning of so many things. We are in search of a better way to live. We are in search of a way to become a part of something greater than what we perceive. Through Nature, we are afforded this possibility.

Once we make it through all the distractions, all the nonsense disguised as normal expectations . . . life becomes much easier to understand. Once we realize we have the power to change things for the better, create a new set of expectations and a new conception of normality, we open doors we only dreamed existed. Once we stop fighting so many of our natural instincts, thoughts, feelings, and understandings, we are transformed into a part of all we've met, a part of Nature, a part of all things. We're connected to all things . . . as long as we don't let go of, deny, or hide the magic within for too long. So dig deep, grab hold, and breathe it all in as we connect our selves back to the power grid of Nature's endless energy.

Two Roads Diverged

More than a decade ago, we stood at the proverbial fork in the road. Since then, we've taken several steps down the wrong path. But it's not too late to turn around. It's not too late to retrace our steps and choose the better path. In fact, now is the perfect time for us to come to the realization we're on the wrong path and change direction. The Hopi have warned us of mankind's fate, as have many other indigenous tribes.

As a whole, the human species has cut itself off at the knees, severing its connection to the Earth. As a result of this detachment from our grounding source, we've become extremely effective and specialized exploiters. We have sold and been sold so many false stories, so many delusions of prosperity that we have ended up exploiting ourselves, our families, our land, and our water and food supply just to afford ourselves a growing level of comfort. Isn't that what we're really after? Being more comfortable by not having to work as hard is the ultimate reward of the American dream.

Often, we are torn. The lives we lead can often be in conflict with the thoughts we think, leaving us in a constant state of ambivalence and consternation. It is no surprise that we express this internal battle as confusion, depression, anger, resentment, or even bitterness. Deep down, we want the world to be how we know it should be, but we are overwhelmed with the enormity of the task of initiating change . . . even though we know it would be for the better. Change appears so difficult at times that we tend to retreat deeper into the shadows from which we came. This retreat is exactly what we must refuse.

While frustration, fear, even anger is a natural response to much of what is occurring on this planet, it is very important we do not continue to feed the fear machine that only inspires more of the same. In my travels across the country, I've discovered many people working tirelessly at creating a better world by focusing on their little corner of the universe. Refusing to be ruled by the normal codes and standards of modern living, these liberators are leading us to a new way of living. A way of living that is focused on Nature, on local food, on healthy food and water and on awareness of our environment. They are daring to change daily habits that so desperately need to be changed so that we can give Nature a chance to heal faster and allow future generations to enjoy a world of beauty and bountiful resources.

Having looked back and learned from what we've done, we shouldn't dwell on the past but rather strive toward what we know must be done on the path ahead. In the spirit of the tree whose leaves change color with the arrival of autumn, we will shed these leaves—our past mistakes—and they will fertilize the earth around our existence to keep us and future generations strong. We will be exposed in the transition to winter, but those who persist will grow new leaves in the spring. How harsh the winter ends up being will be determined by our own preparation, our own strength, and our own will.

The seasons are changing. We must change with them. We must imitate Nature, not attempt to rule Her. We must be shepherds, not sheep herders. We must be guardian angels and protectors, not bounty hunters or assassins.

Nature is begging us to be part of Her again, demanding that we be one with all things. We must remove the scales from our eyes, the straps from our bodies, and allow this reconnection, this union of all things so that the doors of perception can be found and opened, allowing us to walk through to the other side of living. Now is the time for us to kick free from the false desire for convenience and comfort, to unbind ourselves from the restraints chaining us to what we no longer wish to be, and to walk gently into a new life where everything is how we know it needs to be so that all things may reach its fullest potential.

What are we waiting for?

Ho a ka yah ma na
ha - wala

These Words

These words I write are not poems
they are thoughts and dreams
turned outward and upward
toward heaven
these words are my soul,
my torment and my joy
leaving this world
traveling across the universe
and crashing into the next life
where more of everything is revealed

These words
have already arrived in the next life
and once I'm gone from here
they are all that remain
letting complete strangers into
the most significant portions of my being

They are sounds
tapping into the rhythm of an infinite song
and if you listen,
if you are there on the right night at the right time
when the roosters crow
and planets glow
you can recognize the sweetness
of the harmony that lives, thrives, and breathes
behind all our guardian angels' white robes

A *Vision of Nature*

In order to fully understand Nature
to welcome ourselves back into Nature
we must view our existence
as a rushing river
a still pond
or ocean waves crashing ashore
we must look at our body
as a jagged mountain peak
rolling prairie
or dew-covered valley glistening in the morn
we must envision our mind
as a rainstorm,
bolt of lightning
or clap of thunder waking us from deep sleep
we must realize our spirit is the sunrise,
moon's glow
and star's fall
we must hear our own voice in the rooster's crow,
coyote's cry
and owl's infinite question of the night
we are empowered to do all of this
through Earth,
sky
wind
water
and fire

Religion of Nature

The open prairie is my church
the warm southern breeze, western wind,
        and ol' blue northerners are my hymns
if ever I need a cathedral
I will sit, walk, and gaze upon canyons
if ever I need a place to worship outside
        of my inner being
I will travel into the heart of the desert
and up to the mountain's summit
if ever I need to be reborn
I will submerse myself in the river, lake, or ocean
to wash away my transgressions against self, others,
        Nature, and Universe

I need no other human to confirm my faith
for the trees, grass, rivers, and rocks
every last breathing fiber of animal, bird, insect,
        and soil is my congregation
they are my fellowship

Psalm, the Storm

Send forth the lightning!
roll out the thunder
the heavens are parting
mountains belch smoke from swollen bellies
our breaths are but shadows
new songs are sung with new tongues no longer quiet
the kings have all been defeated
no more kingdoms to rule the rules
so come now,
bring the calm after the storm

Getting Back to Our Roots
The Revolution in Food and Farming

> *One touch of Nature makes the whole world kin.*
>
> JOHN MUIR

Back to the Farm

I am the farm. The farm is me.

Once I realized this simple notion, I could no longer deny my sacred bond with the land my family had worked since the early 1900s. Being blessed with the duties of a steward of the land is an extremely humbling and beautiful role once embraced. Having walked away from the farm as a young man fresh out of college, I had struggled at times, trying to convince myself I did not want to be a farmer or be anywhere near the farm. Funny how we try to deny the most wonderful connections we have in this life because of things like pride, ego, misconceptions, or plain old mule-headed stubbornness.

Deep down, I had resented the farm. During the summer months, I had felt like a prisoner there. I had been "chained" to a hoe or a tractor for much of my youth. Confinement was how I had perceived my existence then. Quite simply, the farm had been in the way of my dream to play collegiate football. Ever since I could remember, I'd always dreamed of being a football player. As a non-scholarship player on a Division II school team, the odds were stacked against my six-man high school experience, but nobody outworked me in college . . . on or off the field.

But back home on the farm, it had been very difficult to raise the energy to lift weights and run wind sprints after 15-hour work days in the summer heat. The first two months of each summer, I worked 90-hour weeks as we planted, replanted, protected, and plowed fields for our cotton crops. My dad had just taken on more than double the amount of land he'd farmed before, and it was a stressful time for our family—financially and emotionally. Being the only son, I took on a lot of the burden each summer. It was a merciless grind. At ten o'clock at night, I'd be running wind sprints down gravel roads in the pitch black of night, stumbling over rocks. Other evenings, I'd drive my weary body to the high school field house eight miles away to lift weights. Most nights on returning home, all I could do was stare at my dinner plate before shuffling off to bed. I gained no strength or speed in the summertime despite my best efforts. The rest of my college teammates had been gaining an advantage, while I was laboring in the heat and stress of covering thousands of acres. Unable to attain a scholarship after my sophomore season, I quit my lifelong dream and returned to the farm the next summer.

I was 29 years old when I finally stopped resenting the farm. My own personal pursuit of a childhood dream had coerced me to completely disconnect myself from the farm. Other factors played a role, but that one conflict overshadowed the rest. I hadn't been able to see myself living and working in a place I felt I no longer belonged and dedicating myself to something that had prevented me from living my dream. It's crazy how I thought that farming was only getting in the way of who I was supposed to be. And now, some 18 years later, it is my way of life. It is who I am.

Life is funny with the contradicting circumstances it offers us. It is likely that the majority of young people growing up on farms resent the lifestyle for one reason or another. Perhaps this way of life restricts many of us in our pursuit of other ventures, dreams, and activities. The obligations of this claustrophobic existence convince us to hit the barn door running, putting as much real estate as possible between the life we're expected to live and the one we dream of living. Often, we resent the things that confine us to one particular place. But when we are ready, it is that pure bond between place and person that we embrace.

I was fortunate to get over my grudge and make it back to the farm before my father retired. Many are not so fortunate. A Swarthmore College professor who grew up on a farm in Virginia told me that she regretted ever leaving the farm. "I thought I was so smart, that being a farmer was one of the worst ways to live," she says. "It took me until I was in my fifties to realize how perfect that way of life is. But we'd sold most of my parents' land by then."

Dozens and dozens of other strangers have relayed the same message to me. They grew up on the farm, couldn't stand the farm, left the farm, sold the family farm, and now regret ever doing so. This isn't a case of "the grass is greener on the other side of the fence," but rather a case of individuals having a clearer perspective on life after years of living.

Farm life is hard. But working hard at something we love is far better than working less at something we despise. As we learn more through years of experience, our priorities change. We change. By the same token, there are others who never get the chance to live the farming life they grow up dreaming about. A few childhood friends have told me how badly they had wanted their fathers to be able to afford to keep farming so they could have taken over the proverbial reigns, but it didn't happen that way. Some family farms don't generate enough income to support more than one household so the next generation leaves the farm in search of employment, often in large cities. Sometimes, the older generation must sell out in order to pay off debts. One way or another financial pressure suffocates many family farms.

On reflection, I was very fortunate to have the opportunity

to return back home to the farm. Once I decided to return, I was amazed how powerful the connection was between myself and the land. During all those years away, the farm had grown stronger inside of me. Had I stayed, would I still have resented it? I can't answer that. I only know I had to leave so that I could return with a new outlook on life and farming. Hopefully, this won't be the case with other young farmers today. We can't afford to lose them.

One of the greatest indicators of the disconnection between humanity and Nature is the rapid decline in numbers of farmers. In the U.S. we now represent less than one percent of the population. There are more prisoners than farmers in this country. While we're losing rain forests to the insanity of industrial-scale logging, soybean production, and cattle grazing, we are losing farmers to the quaint predictabilities of nine-to-five office jobs and the conveniences of urban living. Economics is part of it—but not all of it. Some years farming is a hard way to make a living due to the vagaries of Mother Nature, but it's often the mental and emotional grind that wears a person down over time.

While for more than 40 years the tendency in American agriculture has been for farms to get bigger in order to survive economically, it appears this trend is now slowly reversing. In the 1940s the average American farm was 195 acres; this doubled to 390 acres in the 1970s after the advice from Secretary of Agriculture Earl Butz to "get big or get out" and plant "fence row to fence row." According to the U.S. Department of Agriculture (USDA), the average farm size peaked in 1992 at 491 acres. By 2007, however, the average American farm was down to 418 acres.[1] While many family farms still encompass 2,000 to 3,000 acres and some as much as 10,000 acres, we cannot expect higher-yield productions to compensate for the reduced number of farmers—even with advanced technology, more powerful tractors, larg-

---

1. U.S. Census Bureau, *Statistical Abstract of the United States 2012*, http://www.census.gov/prod/2011pubs/12statab/agricult.pdf, p. 536.

er equipment, and the false promises of a wide buffet of chemicals and genetically modified (GM) or Roundup-Ready crops. Rising costs continue to stretch farmers to their economic breaking point. In some portions of the country, farmers are consolidating with their neighbors or other family members in order to afford expensive tractor and equipment payments. Some farmers, particularly in commercial hog and chicken production, are selling out to corporations and end up essentially working directly for them for a set fee to "take care of" the animals on their own land.

The Old, Broken System

In commercial agriculture, we bombard our fields and crops with herbicides, pesticides, and genetically modified (GM) crops without fully accepting the responsibilities and repercussions. Poison is the main ingredient in commercial agriculture's recipe. In 2007, more than 2 billion pounds of herbicide were used worldwide, one-fourth of which (531 million pounds) were used in the United States. Globally that year, we spent more than $15 billion and over $5 billion in the U.S. on herbicides alone. America also purchased more than 1.1 billion pounds of pesticides in 2007, totaling $12.5 billion.[2]

According to the International Service for the Acquisition of Agri-Biotech Applications (ISAAA), we're planting more than 165 million acres (66 million hectares) of GM crops in the U.S. Worldwide (in 29 countries), more than 365 million acres (148 million hectares—an area almost the size of Alaska) were dedicated to GM crops in 2010. The U.S., along with Brazil, Argentina, India,

---

2. Arthur Grube, David Donaldson, Timothy Kiely, and La Wu, "Pesticides Industry Sales and Usage: 2006 and 2007 Market Estimates," United States Environmental Protection Agency, Washington, DC, February 2011, http://www.epa.gov/opp00001/pestsales/07pestsales/market_estimates2007.pdf.

and Canada account for more than 89 percent of GM crops.[3] These numbers are increasing despite the fact more than 50 countries across the globe have banned GMOs (genetically modified organisms) altogether or at least require the labeling of GM products. We have done neither in the U.S.

But many U.S. states are taking matters into their own hands. In March 2012, California had gathered half of the 800,000 signatures needed to get GMO labeling on the November ballot. At least 18 states were in the initial stages of some sort of legislation to enforce labeling of GM foods. So, we could already have labeling in some states as you read this. But these are just the early battles of a long war.

To further secure their political positions of power, Monsanto and other biotech companies spent $547 million lobbying Congress from 1999 to 2009 and another $22 million in political contributions. Our own president, Barack Obama, appointed former Monsanto bigwig Michael Taylor as the FDA food czar. Taylor has close ties to Monsanto dating back to the 1980s, when he was a legal defense attorney for the company. Later, as deputy commissioner for policy with the FDA from 1991 to 1994, he ensured Monsanto millions of dollars. During his tenure in that position, Taylor approved the use of Monsanto's GM bovine-growth hormone without labeling. The growth hormone known as rBGH was known to create severe health issues in dairy cows, even causing puss to develop in their milk. Yet the hormone went on the market with no resistance, thanks to Taylor's position of power. This led to a federal investigation, but he was exonerated of all conflict-of-interest charges. Taylor later served as Monsanto's vice president for public policy from 1998 to 2001.

---

3. Clive James, "Global Status of Commercialized Biotech/GM Crops: 2010," International Service for the Acquisition of Agri-Biotech Applications, Brief 42, 2010, http://www.isaaa.org/resources/publications/briefs/42/download/isaaa-brief-42-2010.pdf.

The revolving door among Monsanto, the FDA, and the EPA continues to rotate in this country while more countries are doing what they can to keep GMOs out of their borders. In the summer of 2011, Hungary burned more than 1,000 acres of GM maize to keep the modified genes from spreading to other fields.

Many studies were conducted by former Rowett Institute of Nutrition and Health researcher Arpad Pusztai in the mid- to late-1990s. In 1998, Pusztai, the world's leading expert on plant lectins and plant genetic modification, announced that laboratory-tested rats fed GM potatoes consistently showed smaller livers, hearts, testicles, and brains. His studies also revealed decimated immune systems and white blood cell structural changes that left the mammals more susceptible to infection and disease. These rats also suffered from thymus and spleen damage, enlarged tissues (including the pancreas and intestines), liver atrophy, and the proliferation of stomach and intestinal cells. These effects persisted after ten days of testing and continued after testing ceased for 110 days, which is the equivalent to ten human years. After 36 years of service at the Rowett Institute, the native Hungarian was fired after making his discoveries public. Few people know of Pusztai or his discoveries about GM foods.

GM foods have genes derived from other living organisms, as well as from antibodies and toxic chemicals. They usually contain both the pesticide gene Bacillus thuringiensis (Bt) and the herbicide gene glyphosate (the active ingredient in Roundup), which are injected into seeds. Seems absurd that GM companies like Monsanto are able to convince farmers and consumers GM foods are perfectly safe for us to eat. Seems even more absurd that Monsanto and friends try to convince us these genes will not go on to poison our bodies. A recent Canadian study published in *Reproductive Toxicology* revealed that of the blood samples taken from 39 pregnant women eating conventional diets, 93 percent of the women and 80 percent of the fetuses contained the Bt toxin—the same toxin found in GM corn, canola, soy, and cotton. Now add sweet corn to that list, as Monsanto has added yet another commodity crop to its GM arsenal.

Some countries like France, Peru, and others have taken a very strong stance against GMOs. Peru passed a 10-year ban on GMOs to protect biodiversity in 2011. Latvia is pushing to be completely GMO-free by the end of 2012.

GM food has little to no taste compared to organic or natural crops. Would we rather eat cheap, nutrition-less food that tastes like the south end of a northbound skunk or enjoy Nature's higher-priced, high-quality bounty that will replenish us with more vitamins and minerals? When we pay less for compromised food, we end up paying more for doctor visits, prescriptions, and other healthcare costs. Think of how many children now have food allergies. The Food Allergy and Anaphylaxis Network reported eight percent (six million) of children suffered from food allergies in 2007. According to a 2008 study by the Centers for Disease Control and Prevention, there was an 18 percent increase in food allergies between 1997 and 2007. Food allergies are also persisting in young children longer than the historic norm, often lasting into adulthood. Everything is linked. We are what we eat, so our food impacts every other aspect of our lives. Why would anyone want laboratory food? Even if it fills our bellies, we are depriving our bodies of vital nutrition and filling it with toxins.

Processed foods contain ingredients such as high fructose corn syrup, corn syrup, soy lecithin, fructose, lactic acid, dextrose, corn meal, soy flour, soy protein, textured vegetable protein, and soy/corn oil, which are all derived from GM plants. Most cooking oils on supermarket shelves are derived from corn, canola, soy, or cotton. Many other foods are contaminated by GM sugar beets. And it's not just plant-derived ingredients—GM salmon are being released into the wild. Just how many foods are contaminated is impossible to know as there is no labeling in this country. Some estimate that as much as 90 percent of corn, cotton, canola, soybeans, and sugar beets are now genetically modified.

Experimental plots of GM forests are scattered throughout the country. Monsanto is now hiring universities to research GM grass and wheat. There is nothing in Nature these biotech companies won't attempt to take over. Driving their ambitions for domination of Nature's cycle are the prospects of vast amounts of power and billions of dollars.

Most people have no clue what GMOs or GM food and crops are. It is essentially fake food and seed. They are carbon-copied seeds that have been injected with genes from other organisms and poisons, allowing them to resist certain insects and withstand herbicides such as Roundup. An average GM seed has a herbicide gene, pesticide gene, as well as antibodies in its genetic makeup. The active ingredient of Roundup is glyphosate, which is proving to cause further damage to not only the soil, but also the livestock that eat the feed from these GM crops. We're poisoning the animals we eat. Cows, pigs, and chickens—they are all eating a 90 percent genetically modified diet. What we are cooking at home and barbequing on the weekends for our friends and family is essentially venomous meat. It is a slow IV-drip of poison running straight into our bloodstreams and digestive systems . . . and did I mention it shrivels your *huevos rancheros* like a cold shower?

Poisons such as Roundup and other glyphosate-based herbicides are losing their effectiveness on weeds. In the U.S., there are now more than 15 million acres that have developed superweeds. These are weeds that can't be killed by herbicides such as Roundup. They've become resistant to glyphosate; in some cases the glyphosate gene that enabled the GM crops to be resistant to the herbicide has been passed to the weeds in those fields. Yet another example of the absurdity of man's attempts to change Nature with destructive methods. More poison is not the answer. Healthier methods are. Nature is building a resistance to our chemicals just as we've built a resistance to Nature's teachings. We continually lower energy levels and the

overall vitality of not only ourselves, but an entire planet by satu-
rating the soil with chemicals to combat our insects, weeds, and
other "pests." Our actions and reactions continue to decimate the
vitality of many levels of life, including soil, water, and air quality
and beneficial insects, earthworms, and wildlife. Monsanto is
pushing forward with GM crops that will resist the much-more
destructive herbicide 2,4-D (a major ingredient in Agent Orange.)
This is in response to the development of superweeds that have
mutated to resist the Roundup herbicide.

As a fourth-generation farmer, I've seen firsthand the destruction brought about by this disastrous recipe of GMOs,
herbicides, and pesticides. Slowly but surely, weed and insect
issues have become more prominent than ever in our area, ac-
companied by more soil degradation, which is also due to
mono-cropping. GM farming is relatively new to this area, dating back to about 2000. So we haven't even begun to see the
real long-term effects. Most GM farmers won't believe this
type of farming is destructive until it impacts them in an overwhelming manner.

Poison is as poison does. It is ridiculous to convince ourselves that the long-term solution for feeding and clothing the
world involves regular, high doses of venom in the form of
herbicides, pesticides, and fungicides. Knowing this, why would
we willingly continue to feed toxic chemicals to our food and
fiber crops? As consumers, we've been lied to about commercial agriculture. In its current form, it cannot support the
masses long term if we poison ourselves and everything else in
the process. As farmers, we've been lied to by corporate agriculture for decades. The majority of the methods we've used
for 70-plus years are part of a gimmick, a sales pitch to get us
to buy more products. The massive amount of money spent on
chemicals has created billion-dollar companies and corporations
such as Monsanto, Bayer CropScience, DuPont, Dow Chemical,
and Syngenta. They've stained our brains through decades of
advertising jingles, spitting out blatant lies through television

commercials, giant billboards, and magazine ads. They've sold us DDT, Agent Orange, arsenic acid, and other dangerous chemicals by the truckload, enticing us to dump it on our land, near our houses, over our water tables, and allow our children to ingest these chemicals via air, water, and food. They know their ability to sell more products depends largely on our failure to educate ourselves. So they use media to convince us that their promise of self-regulation supposedly safeguards us.

To shore their bet, they corrupt universities with false teachings. Monsanto and other genetic engineering companies hand out millions of dollars in grants to agriculture land-grant universities (schools focused on agriculture and mechanic arts) Take for example South Dakota State University President David Chicoine, who joined Monsanto's board of directors in 2009. Chicoine makes more each year from his role with Monsanto than he does at SDSU. Coincidentally, Monsanto initiated a million-dollar grant program for plant breeding just weeks before Chicoine joined the company. From 2006-2010, Monsanto donated millions of dollars to key plant and crop programs at major universities such as Illinois, Missouri, Iowa State and Texas A&M. Those are just the headliners. The concepts of commercial agriculture are designed to benefit corporations, not the farmer, family farms, or the environment. The food cartel—which includes Monsanto, BASF, Tyson Foods, Cargill, ADM (Archer Daniels Midland), DuPont, Bayer CropScience, Syngenta, Dow Chemical, and a few others—has seized control of agriculture from seed to harvest. Farming has been transformed from a personal relationship between humanity and Nature to a complex network funding a select few billion-dollar corporations. See the dilemma here? The fox is guarding the henhouse.

The farmer has to initiate a swift separation from these vampires feasting upon the neck of vitality, sucking the life out of our soil and indigenous seed supply. How do we fend off their plunder? By starving them of the one thing they can't do without—money. Money is their "blood," their source of energy. An informed and courageous public is the rising sun that sends them back to their cavernous coffins, where they're forced to remain until night's shadows return. The only rational way to ensure this planet is better able to ward off starvation and malnourishment is to increase local organic food production. Adopting such a system would drive a stake into the heart of the existence of these blood-sucking corporations.

The commercial agriculture system feeds a disturbing cycle of corporate profits, excessive financial lending, and toxic formulas that increase weed and insect issues while diminishing soil life. Pesticides kill not only destructive insects, but also butterflies and beneficial insects such as ladybugs, lacewings, and vital pollinators like the honeybee. Advertising tries to convince us we're feeding a starving planet, when we are in fact starving our planet to death. This process is slow, it is cruel, and it is effectively ruining the life cycle by preventing energy from flowing fluidly from one place to another. Commercial agriculture with all of its toxins and GM seeds is nothing more than a sluggish genocide of not only people, but all living creatures.

As stated earlier, more than $14 billion are spent on herbicides each year, with more than $5 billion spent in the United States. Imagine if we spent just half that amount on organic fertilizers and crop diversification. But we haven't trained ourselves to plan this way. We're so far invested in chemical agriculture that the easier, less expensive and healthier alternative appears impossible for most farmers to imagine, much less venture to practice. Why is this? Why can't we change gears now? Ego, for one. Most organic farmers who've been successful in raising crops for twenty-plus years say the same thing about their neighbors: "They never ask us a single question."

Jimmy Wedel has been raising organic cotton and other crops since 1993 on his 4,000-acre farm near Muleshoe, Texas. He says switching to organic farming is simply a financial mental hurdle commercial farmers must overcome.

"Many of them think that it cannot be done . . . at a level that is profitable or more profitable than their current conventional farming methods. After all, for most farmers' entire lives, they have been 'brainwashed' into thinking that you cannot farm without chemicals. Just pick up any farm magazine and look at the number of chemical ads," says Wedel. "So if there was ever a doubt, the chemical companies continually remind farmers just how important chemicals are. Ever attend a trade show? Most of the major sponsors are the chemical companies."

Wedel goes on to explain how more rigorous labor and complex marketing also scare farmers away from organics: "Organic farming is extremely difficult—most rational people do not want to work harder. The invention of Roundup Ready crops has made conventional farming very easy. I jokingly say that now any idiot can farm—all you have to do is plant, and then call the spray plane to solve all of your problems, and then harvest," laughs Wedel. "Organic marketing is much more complex. You have to know where your crops are going to be sold before you plant them. If you cannot find organic markets, you may have to dump your crop on the conventional market at a much lower price. Given the historical price relationship of organic crops to conventional crops, most farmers are not willing to take on the additional risks of organic farming for the higher rewards—the rewards for organic farming are either not great enough or not perceived to be great enough."

It is much easier to mock the organic farmer for embarking on a system that requires more time and labor than the quick, easy fix of chemical GMO agriculture. Most farmers refuse to consider the possible economic benefits of receiving twice as much per pound for the crop grown. Traditionally, this is what the organic farmer has received the past 20 years—double the price. Despite the possible economic gain, farmers prefer the more destructive methods of chemical agriculture because it is faster and easier to apply to their excessive number of acres. Despite all the overwhelming evidence and the obvious negative impact on soil health, we can't see the field for all the damn dirt when comparing organic agriculture to chemical agriculture.

These poisons seemingly make farming easier. They have for a couple of generations of farmers. The gravy train, however, is coming to a screeching halt. As topsoil, water tables, and the rest of the ecosystem become increasingly overwhelmed with more poisons each year, the weaker and sicker they become, and the less energy they have to fight off disease and destructive insects, and to resist the effects of drought and other harsh weather conditions. These chemicals breed diseases, creating more cancer in us and more toxic land. This type of environment also breeds more insect and weed pressure. Unhealthy soil raises unhealthy plants. Weeds try to balance the soil by bringing the lacking elements to the surface. Insects try to help the strongest plants survive by destroying the weakest. This is Nature's survival of the fittest strategy. Again, chemical agriculture attempts to override this natural system, thus creating long-term chemical warfare on our soil, our water, ourselves, and every other living creature above and below the soil.

Corporate chemical agriculture knows the formula needed for their success, and they marvel at our lack of desire to educate ourselves. Overwhelmed by our vulnerable economic situation and a whole host of other day-to-day issues that consume our attention, we've hired these same mental assassins to further drug our minds and our fields. Their expensive remedies are designed to keep us hooked on the drug and solely dependent on a system made to suck as much money out of our pockets as possible season after season. As farmers, armed with a series of one-year plans, we want to address these issues on an annual basis. The quickest solution is poison.

Admitting we've been lied to not only about Wall Street investments, the Federal Reserve, and political agendas, but also about corporate agriculture's system isn't easy. It is difficult to wrap one's brain around a century's worth of lies. But once you cross that mental hurdle, everything begins to make sense. This clarity allows us to begin restoring our life and life as a whole.

We can no longer sit idly by and accept the rules and standards that corporations use to run the show not only in America, but in most countries. Governments are mere storefront mannequins propped up in windows for passersby to wave and smile at. Rarely is there a single piece of legislation passed without some corporation having written it or stapled stipulations to the back pages favorable to their own existence and well-being. We no longer have the time or the will to accept the status quo—those smoke screens and mirrors that are democracy. Not farmers. Not anyone. We've been fed such an unbelievably long line of bad bait that it's become rather difficult to fall for it anymore, let alone come near the surface.

Since World War II, we've bought into the false concept of perpetual or infinite growth being possible on a finite planet. Farmers have been fooled into following the dream of attaining larger, more expensive equipment and tractors to farm more and more land. This is, after all, the lie of modernization and progression we've been brain-stained into accepting. Rather than diversifying and strengthening what we have, we're told to get bigger. Everyone has bought into it, from dairy farmers to wheat farmers to corn and soybean farmers to cotton farmers. We've shoveled our funds into larger facilities to house more chickens, cows, or pigs. We've funneled hundreds of thousands of dollars into larger grain silos. We've plowed under bigger bucks for high-tech tractors, spray rigs, harvesting machines, and other equipment. There is a fine line to tread for each farming operation, so the majority of us have ended up being carbon copies of exactly what the industry wants us to be—stretched economically thin to the point of vulnerability and desperation so we'll take the least labor intensive and most convenient economic path each year. Ironically, that path involves lots of chemicals.

Missouri farmer Richard Oswald says commercial agriculture is a gamble as the main source of income, particularly with livestock.

"Livestock farming today is like walking the plank blindfolded—you can't see where you're headed before it's too late," says the fifth-generation farmer. "I think most farmers of concentrated livestock feel they have no choice. Some may even believe they will be better off, but the corporate model doesn't like to share profits. Ultimately, that's how it goes for most."

Oswald has seen GMOs and chemicals become more prevalent around his farm near Langdon. He says farmers have become far too reliant on chemicals and GM seeds to solve their problems.

"Farmers have always called for reinforcements in their battles with Mother Nature. Use of pesticides has been abused, but at least some farmers still wait to see a need before applying them. My ancestors seldom bought things they could avoid using through rotations or other means. With GMOs, the genes are always there whether you need them or not, and the cost is unavoidable because in many cases it's become almost impossible to source seed without them," says Oswald. "We've used up the advantages of Roundup through resistant weeds, and now we're seeing disadvantages to the soil and plants. But those tech fees just keep on coming."

A New Path

The world needs agriculture. The world needs farmers. Farmers need the world to understand our begrudged metamorphosis into this factory-like mentality. Everyone has had a hand in the farmers' demise. A cheap, subsidized food system has forced many farmers to make poor decisions to make a living. The public turned their back on the farmer long ago. As a society, we have come to take food for granted. We treat buying food and eating it like some task or chore we must do. Food has become a commodity, simply an item to be purchased and sold. This mentality must change.

In the late 1970s, when the American Agriculture Movement was strong, many farmers tried to fight the corrupted system. But the people did not join their efforts. Motivation soon faded. Anger subsided. The fight was abandoned. So the farmers felt defeated and believed that nobody cared. Like native tribes a century earlier, there had not been enough of them to fight the enemy's corporate structure. There are even less now, and the enemy is even larger. Now, it is the sons and daughters, grandsons and granddaughters of those farmers who must stand up and fight against a system designed to methodically take us out one by one. But in order to win the next battle, to complete a revolution against the current standards, it will take everyone. This is certainly a battle for all to fight, and a cause for all to stand up and speak for. After all, everybody eats.

Our role within Nature is ideally that of steward, guardian, protector, guide . . . but also that of student, offspring, translator, and communicator. We should immediately abandon the ideologies behind our current practices as manipulators, enforcers, and rulers. We are not here to generate as much money and authority as possible. We are here to strengthen our connection to all living things. In that marriage to Energy and Love is true wealth and genuine power. By focusing our concept of growth solely on finances, we've cut our own throats. We fail to see that we cannot truly prosper over the long term, financially or otherwise, without growing the health of our soil. Our life and energy should be invested in the soil and scattered all around our farms rather than fattening the pockets of billion-dollar corporations raping our very way of life.

It is insane to think we can continue to dominate the landscape with a yearly recipe of GM crops, poisons, and monocropping. We're riding that horse into the ground rather quickly. As the baby boomers slowly fade away, this is an opportunity for younger generations to reboot the system with new ideas and methods. Our new slogan should be "Get real or get out." I envision farms getting smaller, more diverse, and Nature friendly if they intend to survive for an extended length of time. Realistically, few people will be able to afford to farm 300 to 400 acres, much less 3,000. Small farms between 2 and 50 acres will become more the norm rather than the exception. The organic industry will continue to grow as the general public becomes more educated about and aware of the importance of food, soil, and water quality. In 2011, the Rodale Institute—a research and outreach organization dedicated to the advancement of organic farming—released the results of a 30-year study, stating that organic production yielded more than commercial production and was also more profitable financially. That should provide financial incentive for farmers, as well as ecological.

What will the future paradigm of agriculture look like? This will depend on the region. Each region has its own personality due to its unique climate, topography, and resources. But the dominant theme will be diversity. We will see crop rotation; multiple species of animals, plants, and trees; as well as more farmers getting involved with organic fertilizer production in the form of compost teas, mulches, compost, and animal manure. Biodynamics, permaculture, and other natural methods will be widely employed. We'll have to adapt to the changing climate, planting more drought- and heat-tolerant plants that require less irrigation in arid regions. Permaculture design will be key in using the natural landscape to harness rainfall and promote a more natural food forest for ourselves as well as for wildlife.

On our farm, we've eliminated pesticides, GM crops, and commercial fertilizers on over 6,000 acres. Do I think that I will be farming that much land in ten or twenty years? No. But as my dad and I continue to farm together, I'm constantly working toward more attainable long-term goals. We've rotated in several forage crops to build up organic matter in the soil. Dad has completed some major terracing projects over the past 20 years on most of our fields, which help prevent soil erosion on these rolling plains. I have 250 acres in organic transition and more to come. I've planted over a hundred trees the past few years. I mix in acorn-bearing oak trees for wildlife while planting fruit and nut trees for ourselves. We've sowed over 30 acres back into native grass, and

I plan on more. Drought has been my biggest obstacle, preventing me from doing more in a shorter period of time.

Like it or not, cheap fuel is gone. Denial will only delay the necessary transition toward a viable future. Our present and near-future communities must be revolutionized, with local food production at the heart of the movement. The average meal has traveled between 1,200 and 1,500 miles before it ends up on our dinner plates in today's world. With more farmers operating small farms, we'll be able to place more energy and focus on our food, putting a face to the farmer growing it as well. This also keeps our dollars at home, promoting local commerce and a more financially stable community.

For the environment to be healthy, I imagine communities of farmers as diverse as the landscapes they farm. Farmers will also be herbalists, alchemists, entomologists, and botanists providing in-depth information on the healing qualities and origins of locally grown plants and trees. Rather than everyone in Iowa and Indiana being corn farmers and everyone in the south being cotton farmers and everyone in Florida being orange farmers, I see a community of beekeepers, artists, musicians, machinists, seamstresses, welders, carpenters, writers, and other skilled individuals growing crops, foods, and herbs to feed their own families and to sell or trade with neighbors, family, and others.

We must wean ourselves off the corn-based food system. Corn cannot be grown everywhere as it requires significant rainfall. Of course each region will likely have its staple crops, which will be the bread and butter of its local economy, but one particular crop will no longer be the only means of income for the majority. This will create the need for more local infrastructure, revitalizing the manufacturing industry and the job market so that communities can thrive once again rather than be decimated by corporate-led consumerism. It will also be imperative to have a significant amount of greenhouse food production to secure the food supply against extreme weather like flooding or droughts. Implementing aquaponic systems with freshwater fish to help add another element of life to the food-growing process would strengthen our ability to rely on local food even more. But these systems must be efficient enough to capture the necessary rainwater to maintain their water supply.

Where desertification is a real threat, more land will need to be placed in the Conservation Resource Program (CRP) to prevent soil erosion. More grass will be sowed for mob grazing where animals are rotated on a daily basis to prevent soil erosion. By introducing multiple species on the same piece of land, we are mimicking Nature's diversity and the natural migratory patterns of grazing animals like cows. We'll find that certain species complement each other quite well, like chickens and cows, and that others, such as llamas, make perfect guardians for other livestock. Often, our attitude toward one animal is tarnished because it's viewed simply as a commodity and is in and out of a farmer's life within the course of a year. With wool- and hair-producing animals, longevity breeds partnership. So raising animals that produce hair or wool for clothing will sustain a healthier relationship between farmers and animals.

I am adamant that the hemp plant is very much a key to the future success of agriculture and local economies as it has so many diverse uses. Hemp can be used to make clothing, fuel, food, soap, rope, and many other useful products. While it is the sister plant of Cannabis sativa (marijuana), people need to realize that you can't get high or stoned on hemp. It looks like marijuana but lacks THC (tetrahydrocannabinol), which produces the high feeling. Marijuana is hardly the boogeyman drug that causes people to commit heinous crimes against society. Most people who smoke weed simply have a craving for snack foods, laughter, and profound thoughts (or so they appear to be at the time). Decades of propaganda have given it a bad rap. It is ridiculous that cultivating a completely benevolent plant like hemp is forbidden in this country because of its similarity to marijuana. Bottom line is that hemp and marijuana should be decriminalized, as should all natural plants. So, let's get this straight . . . genetically modified plants are encouraged to flourish, but native plants are illegal. Makes perfect sense if you have no sense.

Our global population topped seven billion in 2011. As our population increases, we not only need to grow our crops by working in harmony with Nature, we must also distribute food more efficiently and evenly. By squeezing as much money or crop as possible out of every acre, we are exhausting the Earth and Her resources. We need to be growing our crops vertically rather than horizontally. More perennials and trees should be planted, reducing the need for large, expensive equipment and vast amounts of fuel to power these large machines up and down the rows. More hand labor will be required, thus creating more jobs. Native trees and shrubs will be planted, creating a friendlier landscape for native wildlife. A small portion of fields will be dedicated to wildlife and Nature, allowing animals, birds, insects, and other creatures to thrive. We need to wean ourselves off beef. I'm not saying we should never eat beef, but we're far too reliant upon beef production as our main source of protein, which is causing most of our grain production to be dedicated to cattle (currently, people consume only about 48 percent of grain crops). By becoming more herbivorous than carnivorous, we're also ensuring our longevity.

Confined animal feeding operations (CAFOs) should be dismantled. Animals need sunlight just like the rest of us. Large-scale feedlot operations are nothing more than stagnant ponds of feces and urine polluting our water tables and landscape. Our current food production system is causing malnourishment and pollution due to our "quantity-over-quality" philosophy. By transforming into smaller, more diverse farms we'll be better equipped to put more love, focus, and energy into our respective corners of the universe.

Do I believe large farms will still exist? Of course. There is no magical theory that calculates the perfect size for a farm. Size, shape, and style will differ from one farm to the next. I just see large farms continuing to diminish. Subsidies and fuel prices will dictate the pace of large-scale farming's demise. Those large-scale farms that do continue to exist will have to make good use of implements and machinery that are multi-functional to enable them to conserve fuel—for example, cotton pickers/strippers that harvest and bale the cotton ready for delivery, or implements that cut stalks, till, and prepare the bed for planting. The future of farming lies within a healthier, more natural style of agriculture that is working toward the reduction and eventual elimination of poisons while nurturing more vitality. This transition will not happen overnight. Each farmer and farm should set their own obtainable goals regarding timelines, structure, and size. Being a farmer is a lot like being an artist—we all have our own styles and phases. In the end, we have to be true to who we are and not force ourselves to be something we're not simply to satisfy others.

Imagination, creativity, hard work, and perseverance are keys to seeing these projects through to completion. Focusing on the diversity of landscapes and localizing our food production systems and economies will help protect not only agriculture, but all living creatures in the long run. Nature will heal, and we ourselves will heal, bringing balance to the equation of give and take.

We are what we eat. Food is the fiber of our being. Topsoil is the fiber of our food. Our love and labor is the fiber of topsoil. This precious cycle nourishes our bodies and minds, giving energy to our soul. We vibrate at a higher energy level with healthy food, creating a vibrant circle that keeps the wheel of life spinning.

We need to foster our relationship with Nature, communicate with Her more. Any relationship suffers without proper communication. A prayer is common before each meal in most religious households and settings. The real prayer begins with the seed and how it is nurtured by the individual steward. Also, how it is nurtured in Nature. If the soil is starving, plants cannot fulfill their highest potential. If plants are malnourished, we cannot fulfill our highest potential. It is a full circle. Our actions help complete that circle.

Here are 12 ways to improve our relationship with the Earth and each other:

1. Fear nothing but revere all.
2. Love all living creatures.
3. Respect the Earth as you would your own mother.
4. Talk to animals, insects, trees, and plants.
5. Listen to the elements—the wind, the rain, the Earth.
6. Take long walks. Say little.
7. Sit in open, quiet spaces.
8. Invite peace, love, and light. Reflect the same.
9. Dismiss negative emotions.
10. Absorb Nature's healing.
11. Return this healing.
12. Teach others to do the same . . . especially children.

The poet Rainer Maria Rilke once wrote:

We are continually overflowing toward those who preceded us, toward our origin, and toward those who seemingly come after us . . . It is our task to imprint this temporary, perishable earth into ourselves so deeply, so painfully and passionately, that its essence can rise again "invisibly," inside us. We are the bees of the invisible. We wildly collect the honey of the visible, to store it in the great golden hive of the invisible.

It is often the things we cannot see that determine our ability or inability to progress and accomplish things that the majority find too difficult. Agriculture is certainly no exception.

As an industry, we've refused to listen to Nature. Instead we've been listening to chemical companies for answers. Over the past 30 years, we've become extensions of our tractors and these chemical companies rather than extensions of the Earth. The next generation of farmers must change this.

A New Generation of Farmers

Whenever we think of a farm, we typically visualize a large red barn behind an old white house with a couple of tractors parked nearby. This image usually includes a silo or a windmill along the horizon, and chickens, pigs, and cows frolicking on green grass or hay crops nearby. We also have a stereotypical vision of what a farmer looks like. Typically, an older man with leathery skin in overalls and a straw hat with an apron-clad, grim-faced wife beside him. Perhaps the pitchfork and postage-stamp stare are there too.

It is amazing how many times I hear people say, "You don't look like a farmer." Or better yet, "You're awfully young to be a farmer." My response is always, "What did you expect me to look like?" Farmers are not born with an old straw hat and overalls, and one does not wait to get old before becoming a farmer. Old farmers were once young farmers. The fact that the average age of the American farmer is over 62 doesn't mean there are no young farmers. It just means we need a hell of a lot more young farmers. While the majority of farmers are upholding a family legacy by operating a farm, some are brave and/or crazy enough to tackle this vocation as first-generation farmers or ranchers.

Dominic and Trista Olsen started their own farm near Pierre, South Dakota, in 2004. They operate White Thunder Organics, raising cattle and pigs on free-range pasture and growing grain crops such as wheat, barley, rye, maize, millet, and oats. Even though the young couple had little to no experience as full-time farmers, they were willing to learn as they went along. Most people would have been intimidated by the experience, but Trista says it's the independent lifestyle that keeps them going.

"We are organic consumers who are very concerned about the environmental impact of modern lifestyles, as well as the impact on our own bodies," says Trista. "We can do things our own way, no fighting with others on how we want to grow a crop, treat our cattle, etc. We are free to be as sustainable and humane as we desire."

42

The Olsens are raising three children on the farm as well. While they admit they've had their struggles getting started, their ability to focus on the long term enables them to over-come challenges and accept the sacrifices.

"It's just us—nobody else. To take time off and go on a vacation is hard; we don't have anyone around to tend the animals and help us when the crops need harvesting," says the 28-year-old. "The money investment required to put rotational grazing fence lines in, water lines, cattle tanks, tree rows, machinery, and to establish a home—all needed right away—was, and still is, exhausting. Through this we have learned priorities—establish the homestead now, vacations will come later. After all, this is our heaven. We are connected to the land we tend and the animals that reside within on a very deep level. It's not just about making a living off the land anymore, it's about healing our land and making it into an oasis for all animals to coexist and thrive on."

When they first bought their farm, there was much work to be done because of previous years of abuse from commercial agriculture habits.

"We have been blown away with how fast the land can heal. When we first moved here the soil was dead—no worms, micro-fauna, or other beneficial organisms within the soil for the first five years. The grass was sparse, the soil depleted, and wildlife surprisingly sparse," says the mother of three. "Through our rotational grazing, proper field rotations with beneficial crops, and simply our love of this land, we have turned this barren, sad landscape into a flourishing oasis—even during a drought where others were losing production."

Still, they caution other greenhorns not to be fooled by the romantic endeavor of becoming a farmer without balancing it with some realistic expectations.

"Don't just dive right into it. Read, learn, talk, educate your-selves, and realize it's not a money maker and it's not easy—it's a lifestyle," says Trista.

Anyone thinking of getting involved in farming needs to understand this isn't an easy transition . . . especially if you didn't grow up on a farm. When you are dependent on Mother Nature to make a living, expect the unexpected. Hope for the best, prepare for the worst, and most years . . . expect somewhere in between. It is vital to listen to experienced, older farmers and ranchers simply to understand what they've gone through—the successes and failures. Their opinions and experiences do not provide a blueprint for you to follow, but they do offer some guidelines. When you ask ten different farmers a question, you might get at least six or seven different answers. When all ten have the same answer, it is wise to heed their advice when venturing into the unknown. My basic rule of thumb is to listen to the advice you've sought out and ignore the unsolicited negative advice strangers are always offering. The Greenhorns (www.thegreenhorns.net) is a grassroots non-profit organization that works to recruit and educate young farmers. It is an excellent resource for young people wanting to get started in agriculture.

These days, much more business sense is needed in order to achieve economic success. In the old days, farmers were also expected to be mechanics, welders, carpenters, veterinarians, and meteorologists. These days, add agronomist, entomologist, public relations specialist, and marketing strategist. Marketing is crucial to many, especially small-market farmers and ranchers. They do not have the luxury of corporate commodity groups working in their favor. It's not realistic to set up a little wooden stand and expect everyone to flock there, purchasing everything in stock. People need more than one reason to come to you. Selling one vegetable or fruit simply won't reach the masses. Diversity is key in today's markets, so that a steady income is flowing most months of the year. Those relying on one crop or product usually have money coming in only part of the year. This can make it difficult to organize your finances . . . especially if you've been accustomed to a weekly salary your entire life.

No matter if we've farmed six years or six decades, we learn and grow with the land. Understand that no matter how smart we think we are, Nature always has all the answers. We are wise if we take the time to observe Her tendencies and do our best to imitate them in our daily practices. This will ensure a healthy farm. Remember, though, that a healthy relationship with Nature alone will not pay the bills. It also requires lots of tireless, thankless labor—many hours of blood, sweat, and tears. Some years it is difficult to see the fruit of your labor, and this, too, takes its toll on the mind and body.

Dennis Snyder has farmed since 1969. At 71 years of age, he still gets on the tractor to help the farmers taking care of his land in Dawson and Martin counties, Texas, because that is what he loves to do.

"You have to love to farm," says Snyder. "If you don't love to farm, it makes it even tougher than what it is."

He worries about the lack of farmers in younger generations.

"We need some young guys to keep this going," says Snyder. "I didn't think I was ever going to get started. I was 28 years old before I did get started. Most younger kids just aren't interested because it's so much work. I know it takes a lot to get started, and even their parents are encouraging them to go to college and do something else. One guy can't farm this whole thing. That's what is worrying me more than anything."

All of this information is not meant to discourage young people from trying their hand at farming . . . but it is a reality check nonetheless. Without the advice of my dad and granddad, I'm not sure what I would have done at times. If it takes a village to raise a child, it takes a village and a wilderness to raise a farmer. All this being said, Nature's voice is often the most consoling force we have.

A Young Farmer's Ten Commandments:

1. Thou shalt crawl before thou walk . . . and often crawl between walks.
2. Thou shalt not borrow more than thou can pay back.

3. Thou shalt not live beyond the means of thy average-yield income.
4. Thou shalt honor the land, thy family, thy neighbor, and thyself.
5. Thou shalt observe, listen to, and learn from Nature.
6. Thou shalt not destroy life, but create more of it.
7. Thou shalt not have all thy eggs in one basket.
8. Thou shalt not take the weather personally.
9. Thou shalt need a good spouse, knife, tools, soil, water, seeds, survival skills, home, and sense of humor.
10. Thou shalt not plant GMOs or depend upon billionaire corporations for thy needs.

As farmers, we continually need the support of others to make our vocation financially viable, so that we may enjoy our self-sufficient lifestyles. It is important we support organizations that help us tremendously on various levels. I echo the sentiments of farmer and author Joel Salatin. One of the world's most well-known farmers, Salatin emphasizes the importance of supporting the Weston A. Price Foundation and the Farmer to Consumer Legal Defense Fund. But I also encourage everyone to support groups like Food Democracy Now!, Center for Food Safety, and Organic Consumers Association.

According to its website (www.westonaprice.org), the Weston A. Price Foundation is a nonprofit charity that is

> dedicated to restoring nutrient-dense foods to the human diet through education, research and activism. It supports a number of movements that contribute to this objective including accurate nutrition instruction, organic and biodynamic farming, pasture feeding of livestock, community-supported farms, honest and informative labeling, prepared parenting, and nurturing therapies. Specific goals include establishment of universal access to clean, certified raw milk and a ban on the use of soy formula for infants.

The Farmer to Consumer Legal Defense Fund is also a non-profit organization that aims to:

- Protect the constitutional right of the nation's family farms to provide processed and unprocessed farm foods directly to consumers through any legal means.
- Protect the constitutional right of consumers to obtain unprocessed and processed farm foods directly from family farms.
- Protect the nation's family farms from harassment by federal, state, and local government interference with food production and on-farm food processing.

For those of us choosing agriculture as a means to not only live, but also make a living, these are two excellent organizations to get behind to ensure we maintain the freedoms necessary for us to do so. Getting started as a farmer isn't as hard as we might think. Anyone with a front- or backyard can immediately begin a career as a farmer/gardener.

It may surprise some that any young pioneers are both brave and crazy enough to want to become farmers in our modern, high-tech, hip world of nine-to-five madness that has been the cornerstone of the American dream for over half a century. Indeed there has been a trend for farmers being turned into urban refugees —especially following the Dust Bowl of the 1930s, the droughts of the 1950s, and the neurotic economics of Carter, Reagan, Bush, and Obama administrations. Moving forward, however, we may very well witness a reversal of this trend in this country. The migration from urban to rural and a transition from corporate dependence to independent sustainability appear to be in their birthing process. Don't believe me? Just ask the hordes of destitute college graduates wandering the streets of unemployment. Young people are smart enough to want to dig their fingers and toes into something that is real. And there is nothing more real than the Earth we live upon and are blessed to be a part of.

Marysol Valle is a program specialist and farm manager at Urban Roots Farm in Austin, Texas, where she has helped oversee the day-to-day operations of the farm since 2008. Urban Roots is a "youth development program that uses sustainable agriculture to transform the lives of young people and increase the access to healthy food in Austin." Valle got into agriculture because it caught her attention at a pivotal time in her life when she needed to be grounded.

"My curiosity was piqued, and it just sounded so interesting. It was a heck of a lot better than being broke and burned out, trying to make it as a 'famous' musician in New York City," she says.

Valle's view of farming came from multiple cultures as she traveled across the globe trying to learn as much as she could from the different styles of indigenous farmers.

"The biggest thing I learned from traveling and farming in other countries was that Americans are lazy and spoiled. I grew up with what I thought was a hard life, but I had no idea how hard it could be," says the 32-year-old single mom. "Watching old women and children in El Salvador, for example, work harder and faster than I ever could, gave me a different kind of motivation, and the kicker was they smiled while they did it. They didn't complain about how hard their life was—they enjoyed the precious moments they were given. They were more generous with the little bit of food and shelter they had than any other American I had met. I was so humbled. I saw how they used what I would have considered primitive tools to grow all sorts of lovely things. I learned that you don't need to be rich to be a successful grower, that humans have been cultivating food for a long, long time. I always saw money as an obstacle to fulfilling my dream, and they showed me how far from the truth that was. I was a blessed American, with the world at my fingertips. If I wasted my life away, I would have no one to blame but myself."

The more she was around farming, the more impassioned Valle became about pursuing agriculture as a career to support herself and her son.

"When I started farming, it was the first time in my life when I felt my existence made sense. I was a city kid that got into trouble a lot and had a pretty rough life. I didn't really understand why I had to go through so much crap, and why some people seemed to have it so easy," says Valle. "The whole process of life was a mystery to me, and I was lost. Farming showed me the beautiful process of how life begins and ends, and how all that is bad, old, or dead can become the compost for next season's crops.

"I started to learn to work hard for what nourishes me and to take all the crap I had been through and turn it into the fuel for the next phases of my life. All that I thought was bad or hard was not a waste, nor was I. I had a purpose, just as we all do, and farming gave me that beautiful insight," says the vivacious Valle. "I also was thrilled by how satisfied I felt at the end of a hard day of work on the farm. Knowing that my hard work provided others with healthy food made me feel so proud, and that was a feeling that I had never authentically felt. I had been proud of accomplishments before, but nothing that was so real, so sustainable. That was when I decided I wanted to be a farmer. I knew if I did this for the rest of my life, that it wouldn't be easy, especially for a young woman, but that I would be truly happy and feel like I hadn't wasted my life."

The Yin of Farming

Growing numbers of women are getting involved in farming these days. According to statistics published by *MaryJanesFarm* magazine, 14 percent of the nation's 2.2 million farms and 22 percent of the organic farms are currently operated by women. Women are more likely to run farms adapted to vegetable and herb crops rather field crops (47 percent of the women compared to 33 percent of the men.) They are the largest and fastest-growing group of people buying small farms in America.

Mary Jane Butters is a farm girl through and through. Growing up in a self-sufficient family, she wanted to be a farmer from a very young age. She married a farmer and helped evolve their farming operation near Moscow, Idaho, into a cultural experience for all walks of life. They run a successful bed-and-breakfast; the U-Pick Country Club, whose members are given access to her farm, where they can pick produce, gather flowers, and visit with the animals; and Mary Jane's Sweet Dreams, which sells farm collectibles, clothing, and linen products. Mary Jane also educates people at her Pay Dirt Farm School. If that isn't enough to keep her busy, she's also the publisher of *MaryJanesFarm* magazine, a successful publication she started in 2002.

Mary Jane claims that from early childhood, both genders are programmed a certain way, which influences how we act and react through our adult lives.

"I think the main reason women are being drawn to farming in record numbers is because we're more likely to think and act outside the box, and agriculture needs that right now," says Mary Jane. "When it comes to anything to do with agriculture in a business sense, women have been disenfranchised for a very long time. We don't own land. We don't get bank loans easily. We don't inherit farms. And because of that, we're better risk takers. What do we have to lose? There isn't a set path for us to enter to become a farmer. We don't dream about bigger and better equipment, prompted toward those kinds of goals at an early age by the role models around us. Boys play with toy trucks. Women end up being more people oriented and guess what? It's people who eat."

Mary Jane has become the poster child for creative farming with the multiple sources of income she's been able to generate from the farm. She insists it's feminine creativity and not so much the nurturing aspect of farming that is empowering women on the farm. "Our canvas is blank and because of that we've been over-the-top creative—things like agritourism have female written all over them," says Mary Jane. "My husband, a third-generation farmer, never in his wildest dreams thought about opening a farm stay B&B. At this point, I am the one who has invented how it is we make a living off our family farm." Their bed-and-breakfast was recently ranked by Yahoo as one of the top five places to unplug.

Two of her children with their spouses live and work on the farm as well. She says it is much easier to be respected as a woman farmer these days.

"When I applied for an agricultural bank loan in the early eighties, before I met and married my farmer husband, I was told I would need to find a man to cosign it. I recently made my final payment on a 2005 $100,000 SBA farm-business loan given to me under my name only—no male cosigners required," says Mary Jane.

Valle says women's increasing role doesn't surprise her since most of the volunteers who come out to their farm are women. But she admits it wasn't easy for her when she first began farming.

"No man truly took me seriously. I felt like I have always had to prove myself twice as much to get where I am. Finally, I see the tides are starting to change. Women everywhere are reaping the benefits of a beautiful movement that stood up for women. More and more of us are proving not only can we do this farming stuff, but we are doing it damn well. It gives me so much hope to work with so many women volunteers every day. Women are getting it, the beautiful relationship we need to have with our food," says Valle. "I hope that through farming many barriers that exist between genders can be broken down. Farming heals me over and over, so I believe that it can do that for anything, even horrible gender barriers. Hopefully it can bring us all together to appreciate our unique strengths and weaknesses, regardless of our genders."

For several decades now, more women have left the traditional role of stay-at-home motherhood to pursue careers away from the home. Mary Jane says there are several reasons for this exodus, the main one concerning respect.

"I think the reason women left their jobs as homemakers is

because men and society in general didn't value the contribution. Who doesn't want a full-time homemaker wife? I joke all the time that I want one. But my husband is quick to point out, so does he!" says Mary Jane, laughing. "If you are lucky enough to hook up with a woman (or a man) who is drawn to hearth and home above all else, put that partner on a tall, tall pedestal. I grew up with a mother who was a full-time homemaker. She was always there for us as well as our neighbors and greater community. She considered it her job, and society was much better off for it."

Considering she's helped tutor many young people on farm life, Mary Jane says she is thrilled to see so many young people trying to change agriculture for the better.

"I am smitten to my core to see so many idealistic young people flock to farming," she says. "For fourteen years, I've trained the next generation through my Pay Dirt Farm School, a nonprofit organization I designed to help dot the landscape with small farms again. I can showcase dozens of young people who are now successful farmers on small amounts of acreage. It's happening, and organic has certainly become the entry point for all things alternative."

Her advice to first-generation farmers of both genders?

"Don't listen to the naysayers, follow your gut. Take your biggest, most involved farm fantasy and go for it. I did, and I've never *needed* to look back. It was because I took risks and climbed out on a limb that I'm where I am today," says Mary Jane. "It's okay to go to bed defeated and tired, but when the next morning comes, pull your boots on and jump in, heart first!"

The Art of Responsible Eating

As humans, we tend to forget our bond with the other living creatures. Despite our magical abilities to drive shiny automobiles, don the latest fashion, construct magical devices out of metal, or make full use of our opposable thumbs, we're really no different than the rest of Nature in that we all eat, drink, breathe, and sleep. The magical recipe for thriving human health is really quite basic. Healthy food and water, regular exercise, sufficient rest, and minimum stress are the major components of a higher-quality life. Nature is no different. Plants, animals, and the soil are all living, breathing creatures in need of food (humus), water (rain), and exercise (sunshine), as well as minimum stress and plenty of rest.

Food Expenditures for an Average American Family[4]
(Percentage of disposable income)

Year	Home	Away	Total
1949	18.1	4.2	22.3
1959	15.1	3.6	18.8
1969	11.4	3.7	15.1
1979	10.6	5.0	15.6
1989	8.1	4.7	12.8
1999	7.0	4.7	11.7
2009	6.4	4.9	11.4
2010	6.4	5.0	11.4

If we are what we eat, it's frightening to think what we've slowly been transforming into these past couple of decades. How can we be healthy, vibrant beings if we are eating the cheapest food available and have no idea what is in that food? According to the USDA,

---

4. Economic Research Service of the United States Department of Agriculture, "Food CPI and Expenditures," Table 8, http://www.ers.usda.gov/briefing/cpifood andexpenditures/data/Expenditures_tables/table8.htm.

the average American family spent only 11.4 percent of their disposable income on food in 2010, the same as 2009. That number has been consistent for a number of years. Our government officials have boasted about the abundance of cheap food in America for several decades. It's come to a point now where we really have to ask ourselves, "Is this a good thing?"

Americans are eating approximately 45 percent of their meals outside of the home. What does this tell us? Some stranger is preparing almost half of our meals. Grandmothers constantly baking or cooking up delicious homemade meals in their kitchens is a thing of the past. Now, it is much easier to grab something on the go. Eating is merely something we must do a few times a day. It's done as nonchalantly as brushing our hair or charging our cell phone. We need to realize that what we eat becomes a part of us . . . just as it was once a part of the Earth.

In southern Los Angeles, the climate allows for the cultivation of many more types of food than in most areas of the country. Among the more than ten million people in the immediate area, many are immigrants who prefer the foods of their respective countries of origin. Chef John Keenan says the mix of cultures makes the local food that much more interesting.

"In Los Angeles, you get to experience a lot of different cultures in food, so you get a great mix. [I wish] people could just really step back and treat the food with respect, just have an experience when eating at home or going out to eat," says Keenan. "At Kraft Restaurants, we try to build a story around the food. It should be an experience and create memories for you. For chefs in this industry, we all have some story that comes from our childhood of family cooking, thoughts, ideas that are built around food. Driving down the road, pulling into a fast-food restaurant, and eating your food from one stop light to the other—we're missing the whole idea of having food be an experience and enjoying food and, stepping back from it, enjoying the memory. Eating should be an event, instead of just shoveling food into your mouth to sustain yourself."

Even though they give more consideration to what is being done to our foods from seed to prepared meal, most restaurants and chefs are not as informed or educated as they could be about certain food issues such as GMOs, Keenan admits.

"Restaurants in general have to do a better job of not being wasteful and being aware of the process the food goes through before it gets to our kitchens," Keenan says.

Recent trends suggest many people are paying attention to the quality of food they are putting into their bodies. Restaurants such as Chipotle Mexican Grill continue to expand and grow at incredible rates. Chipotle was rated the 54th fastest-growing business in America by CNN in 2011. The restaurant chain was tops among fastest-growing restaurants. Chipotle happens to pride itself on its use of fresh, local ingredients.

Fast-food joints and other chain restaurants feed millions and millions of people every day. Fostering hectic lifestyles and crammed schedules that find us trying to balance work, family, social, and entertainment activities, we give little thought, time, or energy to what we are eating. Even when we purchase food items at the grocery store, are we really conscious of what these foods are? Do we know where they come from, what chemicals were used, or even if they are genetically modified? Most consumers are not aware of any of the harmful toxins and modifications occurring in our food. There are many things we can do to ensure responsible eating not only by ourselves, but by our families as well. This concerns everyone. Everybody eats. Everybody.

Seven Keys to Responsible Eating

1. Improve Your Education and Awareness—A healthy mind usually encourages a healthy body. It is difficult to know what to do or not do unless you have the proper education and knowledge to support your decision-making process. Knowing what to purchase at the grocery store or farmers market or what to grow and how better prepares you on the food front. Conversely, a lack of awareness can be dangerous. For example, most people have heard of GMOs, but many have no idea what they really are.

2. Grow Your Own—There's no more dependable method of ensuring healthy food for your family than growing your own food. Gardening needs to be more than a hobby, especially for "retired" people. Gardening needs to become a focal point for the family, community, and neighborhoods everywhere. It doesn't take a lot of land. We can grow efficient gardens in front- or backyards, a south-facing window, a personally designed and crafted greenhouse, or in whatever works best economically and physically for each individual or family. In most large cities there are also community gardens that can help provide for the needs of local people.

3. Preserve Fresh Food—This can be done a number of ways, from canning, drying, or freezing to other methods. By preserving our food, we protect ourselves against natural occurrences such as droughts and floods, preventing our own personal famines and ensuring our long-term food supply. *The Encyclopedia of Country Living* by Carla Emery is the best resource I've found in book form. Asking members of older generations is also a wonderful way to learn how to preserve food. Our elders are an awesome source of knowledge. We need to seek their guidance and experience in these areas.

4. Eat Local and in Season—I love tomatoes, but I do not eat them out of season unless we have some canned. We need to be much more disciplined about eating foods that are in season. Learning more about what foods are grown when will ensure we are eating healthier foods. Consuming fresh local food will help energize us and encourage the further strengthening of a sustainable food-growing system. Getting involved with local farmers markets, food cooperatives, Community-Supported Agriculture (CSA) groups, and so on are excellent ways to guarantee fresh, local food. When dining out, try to support restaurants who specifically deal with local, healthy-food growers.

5. Support Organics—Organic food is often labeled "high-priced food." It is easy to turn your nose up at something you feel you can't afford. But how many Americans would be willing to go without smart phones, computers, flat-screen televisions, and all kinds of other luxury items? And these are items we can certainly do without. Food is something we should not short ourselves on by spending less on it. We are what we eat, and we get what we pay for. These days, I certainly wouldn't recommend buying the cheapest food on the market.

6. Demand Healthy Food—This means getting involved in the food movement in this country. By talking to your grocery store owners/managers; to those who run food co-ops, CSAs, or community gardens; and to your local farmers and ranchers, your voice and opinion can help determine the health of the soil and food supply. Stand up and let your voice be heard. Contacting your local congressional representatives regarding any legislation impacting food and agriculture will also help. Also, make a point of supporting groups such as Organic Consumers that help fight for this cause.

7. Boycott GMOs and GMO Companies—This one is vital. As long as we continue to buy genetically modified seed and food, or food containing these items, we give these corporations and food companies (Kraft Foods and Kellogg's, to name just two) no reason to stop producing them and putting them on grocery store shelves. This battle can be won in areas outside farmers' fields. Hit them where it hurts . . . the pocket. By eating organic food and locally produced food, we are sending a clear message: our food industry needs radical transformation.

Locavore Food Movement

Since everybody eats, why wouldn't more people get involved in growing the food that becomes a part of their bodies? Or at least get to know the people who are growing their food. USDA statistics report that farmers markets are on the rise in this country. In

2011, farmers markets showed a 17 percent growth from the previous year (according to the USDA's 2011 National Farmers Market Directory). What other fields saw that kind of growth in the current economic climate? The U.S. saw the number of its farmers markets grow from 6,132 to 7,175. The number has increased steadily since 1994 when only 1,774 were on record. This growing trend is a testament to the increasing interest in buying and eating local, healthy foods. In 2009, U.S. farmers markets brought in more than $1 billion in sales.

Mary Lou Weis has managed farmers markets for more than 22 years in California and has managed the Torrance Farmers Market outside Los Angeles for 20 years. There are over 700 farmers markets in California alone. Weis says that when she first started, only 25 were in existence around Los Angeles. Now there are close to 200.

Even though there are fewer young people on the farms, the Torrance Farmers Market and many other markets continue to thrive across the country. Each Saturday, between six and eight thousand people come to purchase fresh, good quality, local produce in Torrance. Putting a face to the farmer who is growing the food we cook and eat at home helps create a much more meaningful experience for the consumer.

"To be able to provide our community and surrounding communities with fresh, quality produce, and farmers helping to suggest certain ways to prepare a new product . . . I don't know how to say it other than we have quite a love affair here with our farmers markets," says Weis, who is proud of her five-star-rated market. "I am very proud to say that I am a farmers market manager. I want everybody that gets involved in farmers markets to care about that and not to think about the financial aspect of where can I make a whole lot of money."

Many chefs and restaurant owners realize the importance of fresh, locally grown foods and choose to support the local food movement. Chef John Keenan is the head chef at Kraft Restaurant in Los Angeles, California. Kraft restaurants are owned by

Chef Tom Colicchio, who is well known as the co-host of Bravo's *Top Chef* television show. Keenan says Colicchio and Kraft restaurants have long been supporters of local food growers. He buys solely from farmers markets twice a week and has a forager who brings in produce from within a hundred-mile radius.

"Everything we use here is pretty much local. We do bring in some fish and meat that's farther away because we really like the product," says Keenan, who began working as a sous-chef at Kraft Restaurant in New York. "But as far as produce, fruits, vegetables, and all those things, we try to stay as local as possible just to help the community and to support the local farmers. It's something we're really passionate about."

Keenan moved to Los Angeles when Colicchio opened a Kraft restaurant in the area. In 2010, he was promoted to head chef. Keenan says forming relationships with local farms and farmers inspires his staff with even greater dedication in preparing delicious meals for their customers.

"I'm lucky enough to be in touch with farmers, and I think that's a wonderful thing. That really helps you to know where everything is coming from and all the hard work that goes into raising vegetables and fruit—all the sweat and hard work that it is," he says. "By the time it gets to me, the food has already gone through so much. As a final product of me cooking it, it's so much easier for me and our cooks to take good care of the food by knowing where it comes from. A lot of restaurants and chefs don't have that relationship, and that's a shame."

Keenan says the restaurant will often host dinners with some of the farmers who grow Kraft's food. After fifteen years in the business, he knows the importance of supporting fellow members of the community.

"It's a basic concept. It should be pretty apparent." Keenan laughs. "Why wouldn't you put all of your money back into the place you live and the restaurants that surround you? It just seems almost common sense to me. Why wouldn't you want to keep your dollars at home?"

As we have seen, it is critical we all get more involved with our food. This starts with educating ourselves about what we are eating, where it comes from, and whether or not it is genetically modified. We have to read labels at grocery stores, find out the ingredients in these foods and avoid the ones that are likely to contain genetically modified ingredients such as high-fructose corn syrup or corn sugar.

Buying local, organic food as much as possible helps support local farmers and our local community's economy, as well as supporting our family's health. We need to get involved with our local food co-ops, farmers markets, community gardens, pick-your-own gardens, or whatever outlets are available in our communities. More people need to be growing their own food to help support a more sustainable lifestyle.

Many national organizations also need our support, such as the Center for Food Safety, Organic Consumers Association, Food Democracy Now!, and others who help fight important legislation battles. The Organic and Non-GMO Report is a wonderful source that keeps us involved with what's happening with our food. Many books are also available (including my first book, *Son of a Farmer, Child of the Earth*, and the writings of Jeffrey Smith) that inform readers about GMOs and provide multiple resources.

I Am the Farm

I am the farm
and the farm is me
leaving was part of my plan
coming back was life's plan
I never dreamed these fields
could fulfill me the way they do now
it's funny to think what brought me back
a whisper in an open field
my consciousness reaching out to the rest of me
the parts that wanted to fight the idea
that this farm was home
my village
my tribe
my people

I am a man of the wilderness
not of city
not of company
no other man's commodity
I am Nature's son
what I grow, how I grow it
tells the Earth more about myself

each morning and evening
the farm sings a song for me to hear
each chorus a life lesson to learn
so that tomorrow or the next crop
does not overwhelm me at all

Nature's Student

Nature is my teacher
my healer
in her morning light, lifts my spirit
she inspires me
to join her in a dance
her song is sung
by the prairie's wind
the river's flow
the tree's bough
the coyote's cry
the cloud's embrace
the sun's strength
the moon's persuasive glow
the rain's kiss
and the horizon's hope

Today, I'll learn more
tomorrow, I'll share

Dancing Yellow Heads

Dust kicking up from earth
in heart of back-road cotton field
lonesome John Deere rolling across rippled rows
green gears and black tires
covering up faded dirt with fresh soil

Lying peacefully with head on grass
feet propped on trunk
shadows of oak trees stretch on ground
wildflowers dance back and forth
bobbing yellow heads in the wind
stretching for the sun as if they worship
the grandest yellow head of them all

Rural Winter

Melting gray sky crowns Earth with wisdom and patience
there to bestow us all if we look at the right time
with the right eyes
all the universe is calm
wind lies still
whispering kisses through hair of Mother Earth
peaceful chill to further the seasons
when old must die to give birth to new
a time when the aged souls of this life pass on to rest
and children return home only to leave once more
birds perch on sway of wires
no song to sing from their beaks
watching paled earth gain strength to bloom again

Give Seeds a Chance

Everybody talking 'bout
herbicide, pesticide, fungicide, inside, outside
Roundup, 2,4-D, atrazine
poison is as poison does
all we are saying is give seeds a chance
all we are saying is give seeds a chance

Everybody talking 'bout
corn, cotton, canola, soybeans, alfalfa,
tomatoes, potatoes,
no more genetic-modified bye-bye, bye-bye
all we are saying is give seeds a chance
all we are saying is give seeds a chance

Everybody talking 'bout
GMOs, Monsanto, politicos, Syngenta,
Bayer Crop, DuPont, Dow Chemical
corporations selling nations toxic genes
all we are saying is give seeds a chance
all we are saying is give seeds a chance

Everybody talking 'bout
environment, government, locavore, herbivore,
carnivore, existence, resistance, pollution, solution
this is a brand new food revolution
all we are saying is give seeds a chance
all we are saying is give seeds a chance

Shifting Seasons
Weathering the Change

> Wilderness is not a luxury but a necessity of the human spirit,
> and as vital to our lives as water and good bread.
>
> EDWARD ABBEY

Nature's Emotional Expressions

I am weather. Weather is me.

We must experience the calm before the storm to fully comprehend the power of the storm. We must weather the storm to fully embrace the calm that follows its destructive path. Our own personal sanity is tested during the most turbulent of times. It is only by continuing forward into the heart of that storm that we can survive its ferocity and walk into the clarity beyond its destruction.

In the United States, weather patterns are now extremely volatile. Floods persist in the upper Midwest and along the Mississippi and Missouri rivers. Tornadoes have ravaged Alabama, Missouri, and Oklahoma. Drought plagues all of Texas and the Southwest. Earthquakes continue to rumble in Asia. Iceland's volcanoes spit and fume to remind us they are very active. Is the Earth merely going through a cleansing phase—the granddaddy douche of them all? Or are we just paranoid because the Information Age floods us with news of all these events at once? Maybe this is global warming, global weirding, or the Earth responding to "viruses" attacking her?

It is obvious Nature is getting dangerously frisky. What does this mean for us as a species? How are we reacting? How are our beliefs changing? Or are our minds working exactly as they did before?

Many people will scoff at all these theories and shrug off these extreme events. Deep down, however, most people are frightened. I see it in faces and actions everywhere I go. We fear what lies ahead, knowing our excessive tendencies will sooner or later catch up to us. We feel it in our bones. Deep down, if we are honest with ourselves, we fear Nature. We always have. Not everyone, but most. That fear has arisen because we've failed to cultivate our relationship with Nature in a healthy manner. We choose not to understand Nature or treat Her as a living being. We've pushed Her away. Pummeled Her into submission. Enslaved Her. Coerced Her to play by our rules as we've tried to tame Her with technology and machinery, and drug Her with chemicals. We've lost our respect for Nature and replaced it with arrogance and ignorance. We're like the king or queen who has lost touch with the kingdom's people. We've surrounded ourselves with more comfort to isolate us from Nature. We've forgotten how wonderful, beautiful, and meaningful our relationship once was.

Children know this . . . if we allow them to express it. We must become children of the Earth again, true stewards of the land rather than convenience- and comfort-manufacturers intent on isolating ourselves from the wonders of Nature. We must let our spirits breathe freely. Our souls' true oxygen is the magic of a healthy planet functioning in a vibrant manner. We must allow Nature to regain Her strength, to detox Herself from all the drugs. We must be the ones to let Her off the hospital gurney, not the ones who smother Her with a pillow.

Am I saying we are to blame for all the extreme weather? No. I am saying we are to blame for the excessive poisoning and destruction of the Earth that has occurred just so that we may continue to support the con of perpetual economic growth. Am I saying we should leave Nature completely untouched? No. I am saying we should work with Nature, study, observe, and learn from Her. Assuming the role of student would be far more rewarding than attempting to master what we cannot. We need Nature. Nature needs us. It is a relationship of give and take. But due to decades of our wanting more than we need, we must now invest much more energy in giving. By appreciating, nurturing, and loving Nature, we balance life.

Nature's emotions are perhaps best conveyed to us through the varying degree of its weather patterns. These can be as relatively mild as a thunderstorm or a gust of wind or as violent and destructive as a hurricane, tornado, or volcanic eruption. When pressure builds, energy must be released somewhere. And as crowded as the world is today, that usually means many people suffer. With the internet, most of us are now aware of these major weather disturbances and natural disasters. This awareness helps us better prepare for what might lie ahead, but simply being aware cannot protect us completely.

Listening When Nature Speaks

With earthquakes occurring in odd places like Oklahoma (November 2011), we have to ask ourselves if we are the ones causing such seismic activity. The U.S. Geological Survey released a report in 2011 stating that in Oklahoma at least 50 earthquakes have occurred since 1977 near fracking operations in what is called the Eola Field. Fracking (hydraulic fracturing) is a process used in oil and natural gas extraction involving the injection of highly pressurized fluid (along with toxic chemicals) to create new cavities in the rock. The USGS determined these earthquakes were "shallow and unusual" but could not say without question that fracking alone had indeed caused the tremors. However, the British energy company Cuadrilla Resources announced their shale fracking operations were responsible for the two earthquakes near Blackpool, England, in the spring of 2011. It certainly seems inappropriate to blame natural events solely on Mother Nature when, in fact, it is our reckless actions that are creating or at least contributing to such violent reactions.

Anyone who's been paying attention to the weather the past few years will have noticed significant upward trends in its volatility. I will not attempt in this book to convince people that Global Warming is occurring or that we are causing it. However, I do think it is reckless to believe that none of our actions and reactions impact weather patterns. There is far less carbon in our soil and much more in our air today than 100 years ago. That fact is inarguable. But as a farmer and naturalist, I'm just saying here that my experience is that whenever Nature reacts in such an extreme fashion, there is never just one reason.

Texas's state climatologist, Dr. John Nielsen-Gammon, explained the scientific interpretation of weather patterns and behavior in today's world to me over the phone one day: "Especially in the winter, moisture is controlled by the location of the jet stream. If the jet stream moves away from one location, it has to move toward another location. So if one place is getting lots of flooding, there is a good indication a place nearby is experiencing drought."

But even climate experts are stumped by the question of what causes our climate to act or react with such extremes as severe drought and flooding, adding to the mystery and our intrigue with weather.

"It's not obvious why that is, unfortunately. It would be nice to say, 'Aha, this thing is what did it.' There are other factors at work such as the fact that the tropical convection was not as variable as it normally is so we didn't get changes in the jet stream that are occasionally released," says Dr. Nielsen-Gammon. "But in terms [of] whether this is something permanent, it's really hard to predict that. We're in a drought cycle with both the Pacific and Atlantic Oceans having some long-term variations that seem to produce some dry weather in the central United States. Going forward, those patterns will change. There will probably be a stretch of time in the next couple of decades where it will be much wetter than normal in these areas."

Dr. Nielsen-Gammon, who has held the position of state climatologist since 2000, continues to work with his colleagues on various projects in their attempt to monitor and predict current and future weather patterns.

"We don't know with climate change what precipitation levels will do on an annual basis, whether El Niño or La Niña will become more frequent. But because temperatures are rising that means evaporation increases and reservoirs are lower than normal. So that's going to make us more susceptible to drought and make droughts more severe," he says.

We are directly connected to the weather. Though scientific instruments cannot measure or prove this, it is obvious our mood and behavior differs on sunny, cloudy, or rainy days. But our emotional responses can go deeper than that now that we're fed catastrophic predictions. Many forms of fear constantly envelop us. Turn on the news, and the reports are all about chaotic events: fires, murders, kidnappings, bombings, war, and every imaginable act of hate. There is always a boogeyman out to destroy all of us, we're assured by talking heads on the networks. What we don't see are the marketing and public relation meetings behind the scenes or the influence corporations have on national news due to their lucrative advertising contracts with the networks.

In *Weather Shamanism*, Nan Moss writes:

We have it in our power to cultivate a perspective that is spacious, allowing for a necessary role as well as a sacred persona for storms. Storms can shake us, threaten our foundations, and, if we're lucky, wake us up. They can wound us and they can heal us. Any willingness on our part to transcend our survival fears and soften our attitudes toward storms will foster beneficial change for our own hearts. If we can accomplish this with weather that we fear and that is capable of harming us, then we'll surely grow in our ability to love and live fearlessly . . .

The weather offers us a portal, a way in, to Nature. Once we set our intention to engage in a conscious relationship with Nature, we are inspired to expand our focus beyond personal boundaries of self-interest. This is not to say that we are asked to abandon ourselves, for we are Nature, and therefore we stand to gain not only an expanded sense of self, but also a better understanding of our place within the workings of this world.[1]

We're constantly fooled into fearing something, including weather and Nature. It is important we do not fall for this juvenile prank. We must respect Nature's expressions, and we do this by attempting to understand the reasons behind the apparent madness. Is Mother Nature trying to get our attention? Or is this simply another natural cycle repeating itself? Are our own collective emotions feeding into a collective energy that releases itself into the atmosphere? By feeding into predictions of more cataclysmic events, we are simply encouraging such events to take place. By constantly bracing ourselves for the negative to occur at any given moment, we're giving our energy to create such an event.

In analyzing recent weather trends, we can see there is certainly some sort of significant shift occurring in our world. Rising temperatures are becoming more dramatic as winter blurs more quickly into summer. The smooth seasonal transitions of spring and fall are slowly disappearing. In March 2012, temperatures were reaching 90 degrees the last half of the month. Trees bud, flowers bloom, insects appear—all creatures shift along with the higher temperatures. Lakes and oceans are also obviously impacted by this rise in temperatures. Runoffs from snow and ice into rivers are occurring at a much faster pace. Each year, more evidence supports the radical shift of higher temperatures.

How are our own minds and bodies shifting with this process?

---

1. Nan Moss, *Weather Shamanism: Harmonizing Our Connection with the Elements* (Rochester, VT: Bear & Company, 2008), pp. 109, 122–23.

Are we freaking out or simply rolling with the punches? Our own habits must change. It's essential we pay closer attention to Nature's changes moving forward. This helps us prepare and evolve. Performing the same routines based on old systems and weather patterns will prove disastrous. Each year has its own bag of tricks. Our job is to be prepared for the surprises.

Animals sense significant changes in weather before they happen. For example, multiple media outlets reported no dead wildlife in the aftermath of the 2004 tsunami that hit the coast of western Indonesia. Domesticated animals like cattle, dogs, and others were found dead, but not wildlife. Deep down, is our sixth sense also tuned in to these shifts? Or have we suppressed this innate gift through various forms of numbing comfort, like relying solely on technology to inform us of Nature's next bold move? We're constantly looking to science, most specifically meteorology, to explain thunderstorms, hurricanes, tornadoes, and other extreme weather events. Our relationship with Nature is blocked or hindered by our refusal to connect on a deeper level.

Many astrological phenomena have transpired in the past year. We experienced a total lunar eclipse, or red moon, on the winter solstice in 2010 and three more lunar eclipses from June 1, 2011, to July 1, 2011. These are very rare events according to astronomers. I don't claim to understand the overall meaning of these rarities, but with each trip around the sun, I do feel more sensitive to environmental shifts or changes. For example, I can no longer hold a cell phone up to my ear without it causing extreme headaches. Weather patterns have a direct effect on my mood and personality. When I experience pain in certain parts of my body, I taste metal. I seem to be having stranger and stranger experiences . . . or perhaps I'm simply becoming more aware of what I've experienced all along. Some people with arthritic conditions sense a change in weather a day before it happens. Many are becoming much more in tune with their "sixth sense," their "mother's intuition," their "gut feelings."

For many of us, it is difficult to grasp the concept that the positioning of other planets, as well as the Earth's location between the sun and moon has any impact on our emotions, bodies, or thoughts. Yet it has been known for centuries that the moon causes ocean tides, and impacts seed germination, menstruation, and the general flow of life of all creatures. Old-timers will tell you never to dehorn cattle or trim trees during a full moon because the animal will bleed much more and the tree will bleed more sap or juice. Likewise, planting seeds is encouraged during a full moon for higher germination rates. These are just some of the many examples of the connections among the cosmic universe, Nature, and humanity.

"We take nature's power for granted," Tamra Andrews writes in *Legends of the Earth, Sea, and Sky*.

> We see the sunrise and call it science; the ancients witnessed the same sunrise and called it a miracle. We have long lost touch with miracles. We no longer recognize the sacred. The ancients had an intimate relationship with the sky. They lived close to the land and they respected it, because they learned that given proper respect, the earth fulfilled their needs.[2]

By continuing to cultivate our relationship with Nature, we slowly allow ourselves back into the fold of existence. Rather than standing on the outskirts of the storm, it is only when we embrace the storm that we understand we are the storm. When we open our hearts, minds, and spirits, we become aware of our relationship to the elements. We are the elements. Therefore, we are the weather. If the weather is extreme or neurotic, have we not been behaving in the same manner? In our attempts to own or control Nature, we've created a tense relationship that resembles slavery rather than unity. It is the union of humanity and Nature that allows true prosperity. Nature is no

---

2. Tamra Andrews, *Dictionary of Nature Myths: Legends of the Earth, Sea, and Sky* (New York: Oxford University Press, 2000), p. xiii.

different than any man or woman. Any attempt to enslave Nature encourages rebellion.

Working with Nature and One Another

"In nature's economy . . . the currency is not money, it is life," writes Vandana Shiva in *Earth Democracy*.[3] Let us not continue to confuse our own currency with that of Nature. Until we realize our currency is far less important than Nature's, we will continue to wander aimlessly upon this planet with no concept whatsoever of who we are or what life truly is.

Part of our neurosis as humans is our continual quest to manipulate and control aspects of our lives. No aspect of Nature, including weather, is excluded from this quest. Often in pursuit of our own personal interests, we fail to comprehend the repercussions of our attempts to "manhandle" the grandiose structure of Nature. We should be guides or students or overseers—not creatures driven by ego or financial profits.

Nature's method of healing Herself from the damage we have inflicted can unfortunately devastate millions of creatures, including humans. Just ask Richard Oswald. He and his family were forced to leave his family farm near Langdon, Missouri, because of flooding along the Missouri River in the summer of 2011. Rushing waters washed away his entire crop with water levels rising to the floor of their house, forcing them to abandon the place that has been in his family for 150 years. The flooding that ravaged his farm and home wasn't necessarily from more rainfall than the river could handle. It was largely due to the Army Corps of Engineering following a guidebook rather than common sense. Oswald explains his predicament in piece he wrote for the *St. Louis Dispatch* in June 2011:

---

3. Vandana Shiva, *Earth Democracy: Justice, Sustainability, and Peace* (Cambridge, MA: South End Press, 2005), p. 33.

Two reasons stand out for the reasons that our home will sit empty this summer. The first is the revised Endangered Species Act first signed into law by Richard Nixon in 1973. At first, economic consequences had to be considered in plans to protect endangered species.

But during the Reagan administration, economic impacts were excluded as important considerations. That led to lawsuits against the corps as environmentalists demanded a place at the table to help write its manual. Then Gov. Bill Janklow of South Dakota sued the corps to keep reservoir levels higher following serious droughts earlier in the decade and fostered a plan to sell Missouri River water to dry Western states.

Janklow's plan to pump water over the Rockies never came to pass, but unrealistically high water levels in lakes intended for flood control have neutralized flood prevention. One of our nation's greatest flood control projects, one that protected our farm from river floods for more than 40 years, now seems to guarantee a flood mostly because of what the manual says.

That's because competing interests in recreation and the environment have eliminated the corps' basic ability to prepare for excessive runoff by drawing reservoirs down to levels capable of absorbing more.

The U.S. Army Corps of Engineers' River Manual is the equivalent of what an average citizen could expect if he allowed special interests to plan his vacation.

This year, the corps seems to have planned mine.[4]

After his forced summer vacation, Oswald and his family were preparing to repair the farmhouse's basement, furnace, and electrical panel in the fall as water levels slowly receded back to the river's path. They purchased another old farmhouse nearby on higher ground just in case the floods return again in the spring.

"The flooding has reminded me of what I have always known,

---

4. Richard R. Oswald, "My Forced Summer Vacation," *STLtoday.com*, June 21, 2011, http://www.stltoday.com/news/opinion/guest-commentary-my-forced-summer-vacation/article_716d6556-990c-5be6-a148-159e 187031ba.html.

that man's efforts to control Nature are never foolproof, and even the best laid plans can fail when confronted with reality," Oswald, who is also the president of the Missouri Farmers Union, explains to me. "Put another way, what one man can accomplish for the good of all, another man can control and profit from at everyone's expense. The river was tamed for flood control and navigation. Today it's being managed for wildlife and recreation."

Organic farmer Jimmy Wedel says most farmers tend to stay away from environmentally friendly groups due to past confrontations. Strained relations continue today as we tend view each other as enemies rather than partners.

"Most conventional farmers have an anti-bias toward anything promoted by those deemed to be environmentalists," says Wedel, a third-generation farmer. "I think most farmers see them as the enemy—as many of the environmental regulations that have been forced upon conventional farmers have made a farmer's work more difficult."

Lydia Avila of the Sierra Club works firsthand with farmers and ranchers. She believes that the relationship between environmental groups and farmers must be strong so that we are all united in addressing environmental concerns.

"Farmers are the original environmentalists," says Avila. "They rely on the health of the land and know firsthand the importance of preserving what we have for future generations. We must work together to assure that we leave behind a sustainable world, filled with healthy food, clean water, clean air, and plenty of natural landscapes."

Even when specialty organizations such as environmental groups pursue certain doctrines or when tourism lobbyists try to maximize recreational profits despite the negative impact it may have on farmland and people's homes, we can't turn our backs on agriculture. Just as the farmer needs to do a better job of working with Mother Nature, environmental and special interest groups and government must do a much better job of working with farmers and ranchers. We can't forsake one key element of the equation simply to satisfy our own personal pursuits. We have to take everything into consideration. A river naturally follows the path of least resistance, but this is one example from Nature that we cannot allow ourselves to emulate.

In the Midwest, more than 400,000 acres of farmland were flooded by mid-summer 2011. While some of the flooding was unavoidable due to the close proximity of the land to the river's edge—areas that were once considered wetlands—much of the destruction could have been avoided with more careful planning, action, and reaction to extreme weather events. This type of planning necessitates that all groups work together rather than against one another.

Crop Production in Extreme Weather

As awareness of our predicament grows and weather patterns continue to shift, it is becoming more challenging to decide when to plant certain crops . . . especially food crops. One doesn't have to be a farmer or gardener to realize certain crops can grow only in certain areas due to their local weather and climate conditions. For example, cranberry production in the U.S. is limited to northern states like Oregon, Massachusetts, New Jersey, Wisconsin, and Maine. Crops like peanuts and cotton are limited to southern states because they require so many days of heat and sunshine in order to produce effective yields.

While Texas and much of the southwest has endured severe drought conditions since September of 2010 into 2012, areas like the upper Midwest and Northeast have experienced more rain from spring to fall and less winter snow than usual. Farmers have been having a tough time getting tractors and equipment into wet fields, and planting and harvesting seasons have offered much smaller windows of opportunity in which to get the necessary labor done. Extreme weather in the form of excessive rains and cloudy days impacts agriculture, particularly the planting and harvesting of crops when timing is crucial. While these sorts of weather conditions can inconvenience urban-area dwellers getting from home to work, the same conditions can devastate a farmer both emotionally and financially.

New York City broke a 26-year-old rainfall record in the summer of 2011 with 25.3 inches over a three-month period. New York State reported record annual rainfall by September's end of the same year with 52.7 inches of rain, shattering the 2006 record with three months to spare. In early September, flooding from Tropical Storm Lee ravaged New York, Pennsylvania, Vermont, Maine, and Rhode Island.

Rigowski Farms, located in the Pine Island region of Orange County, New York, was hit hard by flooding from Hurricane Irene and Tropical Storm Lee in 2011. The 150-acre farm was under water for six weeks, much like most of the region, which sits at the bottom of a glacier lake and is considered wetlands. Thousands of acres were wiped out. To help farmers, the local community set up an emergency farm aid, raising over $100,000 for local farmers in three weeks.

Cheryl Rigowski had 100 percent loss of vegetable crops planted over 80 acres. Some farmers were able to salvage crops that had not been underwater for more than six days. Most were not so fortunate. Crop insurance is not as helpful for diverse food farmers who plant many types of fruits and vegetables. Most insurance programs are designed to help large-scale commodity crop farmers.

"People keep asking me if we've recovered, but you never recover from something like this," says Rigowski, who has over 100 CSA (Community-Supported Agriculture) customers. "I had to tell my CSAs that they weren't getting any produce at all for a while. There were a lot of deals in the markets this year where farmers should've been, ... but there were no farmers because they had nothing to sell. This has been a test of a local food economy."

Fortunately, Rigowski had her employees plant more seedlings than usual in their winter greenhouses, and the food produced in those weather-protected tunnels is what's saving her financially right now. The second-generation farmer says the flooding experience brought the undeniable realization that she has to restructure parts of the farm in order to survive future flooding events. While most people can't comprehend Mother Nature making or breaking you in the blink of an eye, watching their hard work destroyed by the floods was a cruel reminder of how vulnerable we all are to extreme weather.

The flooding was the worst recorded since 1955 in the area. With over 30 employees and over 100 dedicated CSA members, the responsibility of being such a farmer can take its toll on a person who has everything invested in each year's crop.

"It's like going through a death. You go through a mourning and grieving process. You have so many people depending on you, and you just feel the weight of that in every core and fiber of your being," says Rigowski. "I told my staff, 'Look, I'll get us through today, and I'll get us through tomorrow. And we'll worry about the rest later.' And I got us through it. We got us through it."

Rigowski says many farmers bailed out on her during the tough time. Typically, she has fifteen farmers, but she was down to only one farmer by Thanksgiving. Her work force was decimated by the floods, not to mention the farm's topsoil.

"It's been pretty intense, but we did it. We got through it, and we're here. And we're going to be back better and stronger and different," Rigowski says. "It's a chance to innovate. In the past, we haven't wanted to disturb anything, but we have a clean slate to work with. Now it's all gone so we have a chance to do things differently, try some other type of practices like permaculture on the farm."

With more acreage being swallowed up by larger cities, there is more concrete and asphalt that doesn't allow water to be absorbed naturally into the soil. This also strengthens the possibility of flood scenarios when hard rains fall.

At the opposite extreme of weather conditions is the severe

drought that has stricken the south, particularly Texas. Drought doesn't make as captivating a newsflash as flashfloods and torrential downpours. Drought is death by a thousand cuts. It is slow, painful, and absolutely brutal to endure.

"The drought has been pretty devastating on agriculture," says Texas state climatologist Dr. Nielsen-Gammon. "The cattle population in the state now is as low as it's been since the 1960s. Reservoirs have been hit hard in portions of West Texas, as well as Central and East Texas."

In our region, the only crops harvested were irrigated crops. But many of the farmers of these harvested crops wished they didn't have a crop once they received their grading reports, which determine pricing by different classifications. Even a plant as tough as cotton doesn't perform well in extreme drought conditions and temperatures in excess of 100 degrees Fahrenheit. Well water, even in large amounts, is a poor substitute for sky water.

A River Runs Through Us

I am water. Water is me.

Without healthy soil and seeds, we'd have no healthy food. Without rain, we'd have nothing to fulfill all our hard work. Strenuous labor gets even more challenging when it goes unrewarded. Our relationship with the Earth and all of Nature hinges on the existence of clean, healthy water—whether it be in underground aquifers or above-ground creeks, rivers, and lakes. We are only as healthy as our oceans and fresh water supply.

Most of our physical being is comprised of water. It is no coincidence the proportion of earth to water on this planet is remarkably similar to that in the human body. We are microcosmic representatives of the whole enchilada—the walking and talking ingredients of a miraculous organism. Without water, we're nothing but dust. Without water, even our skeletal structure withers into fragments of a desert thirsting for life.

As June ended in 2011, records were set across Texas for the number of consecutive days with temperatures reaching over 100 degrees. By the end of August, we also had a new record for the number of days in a year with temperatures over 100 degrees. Central and Southern Texas had more than 90 days with temperatures over 100 degrees. Many climate experts believe that when most of the previous records were set, in 1980, it was the eruption of Mount St. Helens that altered weather patterns that year. In 2011, extreme drought is to blame for record temperatures. Rains cool the earth. Without water from the sky, life gets awfully uncomfortable.

Farming is not for the faint of heart, and farming in West Texas is not for the faint of anything. In July 2011, we'd gone ten months with just one inch of rain on our farm. One whole inch in ten months! It's now been over a year in this unforgiving climate with no relief in sight—by December 2011, we had still received only four inches of rain in 15 months. Many creatures are slowly disappearing. Among the few that still manage to flourish in this drought are predators. Around here, that means coyotes and hawks. They're the ultimate survivors, but as the summer heat drags on, even the predators make fewer appearances. Other than that, only desert reptiles such as horned toads and lizards are readily encountered. Wild turkey and deer are starting to come near barns and houses in search of water. Animals become disoriented as temperatures climb over 100 degrees Fahrenheit. People are turning their horses and donkeys loose, but they have nowhere to go and some are shooting these destitute creatures. If this persists, will we?

Where everything else hides in times like this is a mystery. Shade isn't enough. The drought's fierce wind finds you, cutting you a thousand times with finely sharpened grains of sand. Dig three feet down, and the earth is even drier. How anything survives is beyond me. Dry vegetation is perfect kindling, and combined with high winds and temperatures, the conditions are ideal for the grass fires that are ravaging the earth. These fires still persist at the time of writing across much of the south-west United States.

Given my connection to this planet, I'm also personally parched. When the Earth thirsts, so do I. No matter how much water I drink, it is not enough. I feel drought in my bones as it lingers across the land like an Egyptian plague. My spirit does its best to fill my body's cup, but as optimism evaporates, I wither in the shadows' chill. Not even the dark of night can comfort me nor console this gaunt stretch of soil until rain blesses every last thirsting speck. And not just any rain—we're talking about one of those three-day, relentless downpours. An unforgettable experience, like the first time a lover kissed you from the back of your neck to the tips of your toes. A rain that permeates every last cell with orgasmic wonder.

At times, all I want is to lie on the scorched sand and stay there, paralyzed in a meditative state until the rains return. But I must keep moving. At times, I catch myself on bended knees, arms spread outward, and palms stretched upward in a des-perate plea for relief. I close my eyes and weep like a confused child. My body longs for the sound, the feel, and the smell of heaven that exists in all of us. Reaching up into the evening sky, I grab for a lightning bolt to rip open my chest so at least my own blood might give the earth nourishment for a few more days. If only I could lift myself into the clouds and trans-form the water within my own body to quench the Earth be-low. But for now, I suffer along with all of Nature's creatures.

In times like these, a forecast of more drought is a punch in the gut. The local meteorologist becomes someone you despise—an ominous messenger with local celebrity status. The five- and ten-day forecasts are nothing more than grim reminders of further retribution. Fertile soil hardens like a gravel road. Shovels dull in the silence. Backs bend in the emptiness of futile labor. Hands be-come callous and bleed, unable to grasp anything, particularly the cruelty of the situation. The horizon only a bubbly illusion melting into the promise of tomorrow's existence.

It is a hollow feeling that leaves one helpless, emotionally paralyzed. Motivation wavers in the mornings. Inspiration flees in the early afternoons. Still, like all farmers and other creatures, I must press on with as much zeal as I can muster in barren times. My knees buried in the earth, I search the skies for answers, for redemption, for any sign of hope that might transform itself into a rainstorm, a bolt of lightning, a roll of thunder, a rain cloud, a shower, a sprinkle, a mist, a heavy fog . . . just a single drop of rain to find me and kiss me upon the cheek so I might smile and sigh in great confidence that a fulfilling rain will soon come our way.

For a clearer perspective on the importance of water for life, go one day without drinking anything. Try to make it three days without water. Before the first day is over, one comes to a very simple and grand realization—water is everything. Without it, our physical forms cease to exist. Parched lips, cracked skin, swollen tongue, numbed body, dry throat—all beg for relief, just one drop to ease this misery.

All the money in the world cannot quench our thirst if no clean water is to be found. By ignoring and abusing our most precious resource, we are denying the part of our selves that is the most crucial, the most important aspect of what is pure, what is true, and what is absolutely fundamental for our own personal survival. We take water for granted. We assume it will always be available and plentiful, because it has been so easily accessible for so many years.

A family member once asked me, "We've had water here for a hundred years, so why do you want to spend so much money and time collecting rainwater?" In fairness, the question was asked before the year-long drought. It is easy to scoff at such a question, but it is unfortunately the attitude of the vast majority of people in America and in many other parts of the world. This is an arrogance that has plagued our species for the better part of an entire century. Whenever we have plenty of something, we give little to no consideration to the possibility of it ever running out . . . until it is too late.

An older farmer I know once made a comment that said

much about human behavior and attitudes toward living. We were speaking about the Ogallala Aquifer levels. Surrounded by oil wells, he raised his arms in open surrender and said, "Our water tables are dropping, but I'm going to keep pumping it out of the ground. If I don't, it's just going to get ruined by these oil companies. All this fracking will contaminate our underground water sooner or later."

Herein lies our conundrum, and I totally get what this farmer was saying. However, while I agree that the excessive amount of unregulated oil industry activity and fracking's destructive methods are decimating our water supplies, I know commercial agriculture's impact is even more significant. Through livestock and crop irrigation, agriculture consumes 80 to 85 percent of the country's water supply.

Dr. Kevin Mulligan, associate professor at Texas Tech University and director of the Center for Geospatial Technology, says it is tricky to try to point a finger at those responsible for the rapid decline of aquifer levels. "An economist friend of mine had an interesting take on this. He said, 'From a purely economic point of view, there's no rationale for conserving water unless you know you can make more money on it later.' And that's true. Why conserve water if after you pass away, someone else is going to come along and pump it and make money?" says Mulligan. "Having it sit down there and not using it, what does that accomplish? If that incentive is not there, then what's anyone's incentive for conserving? It's a brutal way at looking at things, but there's probably some truth to it. If a farmer is sitting there and decides he really wants to conserve water, but his neighbors continue to pump, then he's going to lose his water anyway. So, I don't see a way out of this."

Our inability to balance what is enough to make a living versus taking as much as we possibly can has plagued our species through the centuries. From Christopher Columbus's quest for cotton and gold to Spanish Conquistadors thirst for more gold to enrich the kingdoms of Spain, England, France, and Italy, all searching to expand their territories and resources, to the present day when we continue to utilize resources for our own financial gain. And we consume these resources much faster as time progresses with the help of technology and machinery.

Whether it has been water, gold, buffalo, timber, oil, or whatever we've needed, we've convinced ourselves that we must harvest as much as humanly possible before someone else gets it. We are like children at a dinner table, consuming everything down to the bone as if to win some sort of prize for gluttony. Rather than coming up with 50-year plans, we have me-now plans. Considering our impact on Nature, that has proven to be extremely dangerous. In the six decades following World War II, we have consumed more than 50 percent of this planet's resources. We've proven that we don't know our limitations. Excess is the method of our madness. Sometimes to know what is enough, we have to know what is too much. But with Nature's most precious commodities, that is playing with fire. I have no remedy for this ailment. We all have choices to make in life, whether motivated by money or not. It is up to us as individuals to realize and understand not only the short-term benefits for ourselves, but also the long-term effects on everything and everyone once we are gone. Being the richest person in the cemetery doesn't hold a whole lot of water.

What the Frack?

Fracking, or hydraulic fracturing, has increasingly become more of a problem over the past decade as it has been known to contaminate water wells and our underground aquifers. Oil companies inject a high-pressure mix of water, sand, and a cocktail of VOCs (volatile organic compounds) that allow the oil or natural gas to flow more freely to the surface. Over 80,000 pounds of chemicals are injected into the Earth's crust for each well, and 70 percent of these nonbiodegradable chemicals remain in the Earth. These toxic chemicals seep into our water supply.

They include benzene, toluene, ethylbenzene, and xylene. About 3.5 million gallons of water is used to frack each well and some wells are fracked multiple times. So the process also generates a major draw on our water supply.

ExxonMobil's CEO Rex W. Tillerson stated in 2010 at a congressional hearing on drilling that "there have been over a million wells hydraulically fractured in the history of the industry, and there is not one, not one, reported case of a freshwater aquifer having ever been contaminated from hydraulic fracturing. Not one." Ironically, in December of 2011, government officials directly linked hydraulic fracturing to water contamination for the first time in the U.S. The case involved the community near Pavillion, Wyoming, where 11 different water wells were contaminated, and it was reported that the water had turned black and smelled and tasted bad. Health issues believed to be linked to the contaminated water were reported too.

The 2010 documentary *Gasland* by Josh Fox highlights several homeowners and ranchers whose water wells were contaminated by fracking after they had leased their land to Halliburton for natural gas drilling. Individuals were actually able to set the water coming out of their faucets on fire. They could no longer wash clothes or take baths, let alone drink their own water. Livestock were dying from drinking contaminated water. They discovered that cash is a poor substitute for water.

Amy Mall is a senior policy analyst for the NRDC (National Resource Defense Council) and has intensively covered fracking and water contamination cases in the U.S. At least 11 states have multiple reports linking water contamination to nearby fracking. Having worked for the NRDC for more than a decade, Mall says it is extremely difficult to provide indisputable evidence in these cases. "There are many cases across the United States where drinking water is contaminated and they link it to nearby fracking. Sadly, these cases have never been investigated by governing agencies so we don't know exactly what the link is, but there is enough evidence [that] we should be concerned," says Mall. "We need a new wave of research to better understand the threat to communities and drinking water so we can reduce the risks."

In 1982, our family's personal water well was contaminated by a local rig drilling for oil on neighboring land. The oil company never accepted responsibility for the contamination, but they did cover the drilling costs for a new water well. In February of 2012, I noticed two spots on our family farm where puddles of water formed on top of the ground. The soil has been bleached white, and nothing will grow. I called the Texas Railroad Commission, which regulates the oil industry. An inspector viewed the site. It is still under investigation, but is believed to be either a leak from an old oil well that was not capped properly or an old sludge pit "sweating" up to the top. This dead zone is a small area, covering roughly 100 square feet. Hopefully, it will be taken care of quickly. This means either the original oil company or the state will have to foot the bill for digging beneath the surface and recapping the old well.

This is a microcosm of an environmental calamity that can occur even decades after oil activity has ceased. Particularly as oil and natural gas activity has increased in the U.S., we need to push for stronger regulation of water contamination and legislation that holds oil companies libel for damages.

Raising Awareness of Our Aquifer Levels

In 1950, just over three million acres were irrigated in Texas. In 2000, the number of irrigated acres was 6,490,000. In half a century, we have doubled our irrigated acreage in some of the most desolate, arid parts of the nation. More than 61 million acres are irrigated in the U.S., with California leading the way.

Some states use more water per day than others due to less efficient methods, such as flood irrigation. But will the water to do this always be there? Will it be there in as little as 15 or 20 years?

Percentage of Total U.S. Irrigation Water Withdrawals during 2005[5]

1. California—19%
2. Idaho—13%
3. Colorado—10%
4. Arkansas—7%
5. Nebraska—7%
6. Montana—7%
7. Texas—6%

The Ogallala Aquifer is the largest reservoir of water in North America and covers more than 174,000 square miles in eight different states (South Dakota, Wyoming, Nebraska, Kansas, Colorado, Oklahoma, New Mexico, and Texas). Roughly 27 percent of the total irrigated land in the United States sits atop the Ogallala, accounting for more than 100 million acres.

While many think we can never run out of water on the Great Plains, research shows otherwise. Although researchers believe we've depleted just over 10 percent of the entire Ogallala, that statistic is misleading since most of the aquifer resides under the Sandhills in Nebraska, and this portion is not being pumped. Dr. David Brauer, the program manager for the USDA's Ogallala Aquifer Program, says we've used up to 67 percent of the Ogallala in places since the 1950s. North of the Canadian River, the Ogallala is plentiful. But south of the river's path, it is a different story. The Canadian River is lower in elevation, so the water in the aquifer empties into the river and is carried down its path.

Brauer admits their data may not be completely accurate as much is unknown about how water levels fluctuate in underground wells. "This brings up a whole other question. If how we are collecting data on the aquifer does not truly accurately

---

5. U.S. Geological Survey, "Water Questions & Answers: Which States Irrigated the Most?" http://ga.water.usgs.gov/edu/qa-usage-stateirr.html.

measure the water level, there may very well be less water than we estimate," he says.

If the figures are overestimated, and considering the severity of the current drought, continuing excessive irrigation, and increasing oil-well drilling, we are probably living on borrowed water already, despite the grandiosity of the Ogallala. Sound ridiculous? Water has already been depleted in isolated areas.

"In some areas, water levels seem to be maintaining their levels. Other places such as Happy, Texas, have already depleted most of their water wells," says Brauer.

Brauer also says that many farmers are adding more irrigated acres once they realize they have enough water to do so. Rather than being satisfied with a small area of irrigation, most farmers want to irrigate as many acres as they possibly can. In past years, this approach has paid off economically. But as the drought persists, water wells are dropping to all-time lows. Pivot irrigation systems can't pump enough water on crops suffering through 50 or more days of 100-degree-plus temperatures and less than two inches of rainfall. In 2011, wells were simply exhausted in order to keep crops alive.

Given all these daunting predictions regarding our near future, what is Brauer's advice to young farmers? "You'd better learn how to farm without irrigation," he says.

The Future of Large-Scale Irrigation

With the global population surpassing seven billion people in 2011, the human race continues to multiply at an exceedingly high rate. In 0 AD, it is estimated there were 300 million people on the planet. Fast forward to 1800, and we topped one billion people. Roughly 127 years later, in 1927, we had doubled to more than two billion. Yet, it took only 72 more years for us to triple that number.[6]

---

6. Susan K. Lewis, "Human Numbers Through Time," Nova, April 20, 2004, http://www.pbs.org/wgbh/nova/earth/global-population-growth.html.

Global Population (in Billions)	Time Span between Billions	Year Reached
1	—	1800
2	100 years	1927
3	30 years	1960
4	15 years	1974
5	14 years	1987
6	10 years	1999
7	12 years	2011

Our population growth trends are slowly decreasing, but it is estimated we will have eight billion people on the planet by 2026.[7] Another billion people to feed, clothe, and water. Our current methods of crop production, involving excessive irrigation, will not be adequate as water tables shrivel and the population expands. The rubber band will snap at some point. That snapping point is in our near future.

Dennis Snyder has seen farmland managed with and without center-pivot irrigation. Commonly, a center pivot will irrigate a 160-acre circle. This system is the backbone of irrigation farming for commercial agriculture on the High Plains of West Texas. Snyder grew up on a farm near Lamesa, Texas, working for his dad before striking out on his own in 1969.

"The only irrigation in [the] early fifties was on one farm in Snyder's area of Dawson County. The 1960s brought on the irrigation in West Texas. Of course I've been irrigating ever since I started, but everything has been pretty steady until this past year. This year—2011—has taken its toll on the water," says Snyder. "You hope you get some rain and usually you do, but we never did this year. These wells, you can turn them on for two or three days, but because we've constantly watered we

---

7. United States Census Bureau, International Data Base, Total Midyear Population for the World: 1950–2050, http://www.census.gov/population/international/data/idb/worldpoptotal.php.

can't keep up with that. We'd dry this country up if we had to do this every year. We have to depend on Mother Nature and the good Lord for our moisture."

Even the most optimistic farmer has to wonder what will come of irrigated land in the near future with rising temperatures and severe droughts becoming more common.

"Since cotton [prices] got so high, you think you need irrigation since dryland [nonirrigated farming] is so iffy so much of the time. It wouldn't take so long to pay for an irrigated farm years ago, but these days I'm not so sure that's the way to go because it's so expensive to get started," says the 70-year-old Snyder. "I know lots of land around here used to have better-quality water and more of it. These days a lot of it is a little on the salty side so you have to add calcium to your fertilizer to keep your soil from getting so hard. There's still lots of good water around too."

Scientists who've been studying the Ogallala insist that irrigation agriculture as we've known it in these parts will slowly but surely become a thing of the past. Dr. Kevin Mulligan says we're mining the Ogallala Aquifer like we have other resources in the past—as if its reserves of water were infinite. It is, in fact, slowly being dissipated.

"My biggest area of interest is the decline of the aquifer itself. We see a pretty consistent decline in the aquifer. If those trends continue, we see the aquifer being depleted down to 30 feet," says Mulligan, who has data going back to 1990. "Once you get down to 30 feet of saturated thickness, it gets to a point where you can't support the center pivot. So, a well maybe that was producing 450 to 500 gallons per minute 15 years ago, now that well is only producing 100 or 150. So there just isn't enough water. Now, we're seeing several wells to support a center pivot. Once the aquifer is drawn down to 30 feet, that basically is the end of large-volume center pivot."

Snyder has experienced declining wells in Dawson County. His wells are generally 185 to 200 feet deep. But some of Snyder's wells go as deep as 265 feet to get the desired pressure of 450 gallons per minute for pivot systems.

"Everybody sure has a lot more wells than they used to. I don't know if that's going to be the answer anymore. After you drill four or five wells on 160 acres, I don't know that it helps you a whole lot more to drill another one because you're probably just sucking your water down dryer," says Snyder.

"When we project out into the future given current trends, within 20 or 30 years, I can't see how this region can support center-pivot irrigation. Now some people will convert over to drip irrigation but I think we're looking at . . . not an end to . . . but a dramatic reduction in center-pivot irrigation," says Mulligan. One of the goals of conservation efforts is to ensure that the aquifer is at 50 percent capacity in a few decades. "With current trends," Mulligan says, "I don't see how they're going to attain that." Unless there's a dramatic reduction in usage, much more than half will be consumed in that time.

Mulligan explains that it is impossible to predict or measure the current drought situation as it takes several years for recharge water from rainfall to reach the aquifer. Draw down is happening faster (as much as 80 feet in 15 years or 5 feet per year) in Castro and Parmer counties, where a lot of corn is raised—a crop that requires more water. There is also much more water in those counties.

Mulligan says farmers are very aware of what their personal wells are doing from one year to the next. Where there is more water, land prices are more expensive. So farmers in those areas use more water in order to pay off land loans and other expenses in a shorter period of time. It is basic mathematics. But the longevity of the aquifer suffers in the equation.

"What I see is the aquifer being effectively mined. It's no different than an oil field. Oil field companies go in, pump the oil, and when the oil runs out they move on. I don't see much difference," says Mulligan. "There's very little recharge. Down in this part of the Ogallala, it's effectively mining, and it's not going to recharge."

Through the history of the Southern Plains, Mulligan traces how extreme shifts in culture and weather patterns have altered the region. He sees the same shifts happening in the near future.

"If you look at the history of this region before any white settlement, it was bison and Indians, right? Then we removed the bison and Indians," says Mulligan. "Then what followed? The economy was based on cattle. You had huge cattle ranches, but with the huge drought in the late 1800s and the fencing . . . basically that decimated the cattle industry. The economy switched from an economy based on cattle to an economy based on dryland agriculture. That carried on to the dust bowl and that kind of brought a lot of dryland agriculture to a halt. As we get into 1940s and World War II and the 1950s, we got into irrigation agriculture. I just see the aquifer being mined. It's not going to get dry, but it's going to get to the point where it can't support irrigation agriculture anymore. We'll see a slow transition back into dryland agriculture."

In certain areas like Terry County, the decimation of the aquifer is already happening. Irrigation farmers are already using just half their pivots and rotating the other half of their acreage each year.

"I wish I could see into the future. All we can do is use the tools we have today and kind of project out and make some guesses," says Mulligan. "I guess I'm not optimistic about conserving the aquifer. I don't see a mechanism, and I don't really blame anybody either. It's hard to say, 'Oh, you shouldn't be doing this.' Who am I to tell the producer to not do this? He's got payments to make, and the banks breathing down his neck."

Billionaire investors such as T. Boone Pickens have been well ahead of the curve, realizing the financial significance of water's future. In 2011, Pickens's company Mesa Water Inc. sold water rights to 210,000 acres in West Texas for $103 million to the Canadian River Municipal Water Authority. The deal is estimated to involve more than four trillion gallons of water, which should keep West Texas going into the 22nd century. Pickens abandoned his original plan of building a pipeline to Dallas, which would've cost over $3 billion.

Water should not be treated as the latest trendy commodity. It should be treated with respect and reverence for what it truly is— necessary for our survival. So the big question is how do we feed a growing population while reducing our impact on our underground water supply? It starts with one crop that can be harvested in any and every region across the planet—rainwater.

By harvesting rainwater, we are utilizing a viable resource that often goes wasted, spilling off our rooftops and washing away soil below. Imagine if every single household and business were equipped with rainwater-harvesting systems, catching every last drop. Imagine if barns and houses on every farm were equipped with rainwater-harvesting systems. We could be harvesting billions and billions of gallons each year across the state of Texas, let alone the entire country. Just 10,000 square feet of roof can net more than 62,000 gallons from a mere ten inches of rainfall. Imagine if cities were forward thinking enough to enhance their out-of-date water-drainage infrastructure to maximize rainfall collection, employing natural methods that would help ensure the health of the rivers, streams, and creeks in nearby urban areas. Our watersheds are vulnerable in so many areas of modern living, it is imperative we not only protect, but also enhance municipal and rural infrastructure to create a healthier environment for the future.

Philly Sheds Light on Water Usage

One U.S. urban area that is definitely addressing watershed issues is the City of Philadelphia. The Philadelphia Water Department (PWD) chose to be extremely proactive rather than waiting to be reactive to the rapid changes occurring in urban existence in relation to rising populations. As more construction occurs, there is less and less uncovered earth, and this further complicates management of storm-water runoff and drainage on city streets. As the city and surrounding areas found out in 2011, heavy rainfall is occurring with record frequency.

The 1996 Safe Drinking Water Amendment Acts were passed in the U.S. for all American cities to assess potential sources of contamination to all source water supplies in the country. The City of Philadelphia took this matter seriously. In 2002, they passed the Source Water Assessment (SWA) and the Source Water Protection Plan (SWPP) in order to protect their water sources. According to the Philadelphia Watershed Project's website, at the heart of the plan's recommended action is "a holistic watershed approach that recognizes the interconnectedness between source water protection concerns, upstream land and water use, and the need to maintain a healthy aquatic ecosystem."

Lesley Saliga moved to Philadelphia to work as a volunteer through Americorp Vista. The Chicago native acted as a community liaison representative for the TTF (Tookany/Tacony Frankford) Watershed Partnership, which works closely with the PWD on the Green City, Clean Waters Program. Saliga's duties included bringing people out to do cleanups along the streams, and to plant trees and various plants. She also helped to educate people about the city's current water drainage and pollution issues. The old system routes the city's sewage and storm water into riverways through old pipes.

"The main issue is that there's too much water in the system. Every time it rains, the combination of excess water is too much for the old system to handle," says Saliga. "All the waste going down these drains as well as industrial waste is going into the waterways. There is a lot of pollution going into the rivers. We're trying to bring back the ecosystem. The main focus is the green infrastructure."

The cooperation of the community through volunteer labor was and is crucial for this project to succeed. It is a perfect example of people pulling together with a common goal and being inspired to improve not only their neighborhoods, but the environment as well. Saliga says they were able to accomplish much with a shoestring budget of $1,800 in 2011. "What we're doing is putting together all the skills necessary to do these projects. We're able to really make those connections, build those relationships, and it's a model, a demonstration really," says the DePaul University graduate. "It's taking all of these different communities and organizations to complete a project with very little funding. We've already been able to do cleanups, training volunteers with gardening and landscaping skills. It's an amazing partnership with over 20 organizations with very little money. We're just using our resources to accomplish our goals."

Philadelphia is already working to address the problem of rising sea levels. This will bring salt water farther inland and into waterways such as the Delaware River. This river, combined with the Schuylkill River, supply all of the city's drinking water. The Philadelphia Water Department's water treatment plant currently treats more than 250 million gallons of water each day for its citizens.

Joane Dahme is the general manager of public affairs for the PWD. She says the project is a huge part of the city's overall vision of creating a healthier environment for not only its citizens, but for Nature as well. They are putting their money where their mouth is. The city is investing between $100 and $125 million over the next 25 years into stream restoration, hoping to achieve 85 percent pollutant-load capture by 2036.

"Although it is not a regulatory requirement under the Green City, Clean Waters plan, it is an important element of PWD's Green City, Clean Waters vision," says Dahme. "We believe that stream restoration complements green storm-water infrastructure management and that in order to meet our ultimate goals of fishable, swimmable, beautiful, and accessible waterways, it only makes sense for us to incorporate stream restoration/stabilization as well. The restoration of streams means improved habitat and increased aquatic resources in streams that are stabilized. These benefits will further improve the conditions of the stream and the experience of the park user."

Assessing other possible water contamination concerns, the city acknowledged several other issues such as forest clearing and development; agriculture runoff, since 25 percent of the land along the Delaware and Schuylkill rivers is used for agriculture; spills and accidents, such as oil spills, sewage leaks and fish die-offs; treated wastewater effluent; improper disposal of trash/waste; pharmaceuticals, as more than 20 percent of Americans are on some type of antidepressant or medication and these toxins are released into the sewage system; and wildlife pollution, as many geese and other wildlife gather near the rivers.

Philadelphia has already begun construction of rainwater gardens in various communities to help take pressure off storm-water drainage and river pollution. They expect to have approximately 237 "green street" blocks constructed over the next two years. Workers and volunteers started installing green streets equipped with storm-water tree trenches, storm-water planters, and storm-water bumpouts as well as porous asphalt in the fall of 2011.

"Many of the green streets are in front of schools, recreation centers, and parks, therefore providing us with opportunities to build stronger partnerships with Philadelphia Parks and Recreation and the School District of Philadelphia," Dahme says. "These sites also further our ability to offer educational programming to the students at the schools and users of the recreation centers. The programming offered incorporates topics such as watershed management, storm-water runoff and green storm-water infrastructure. Ultimately, we envision these communities (students, staff, and civic groups) as adopters of the green storm-water infrastructure. As such, we are also currently developing a Green City, Clean Waters Ambassador program, in addition to a Green Streets Adoption Guide."

The PWD is also constructing green streets when replacing streets following major sewer work. They are working in conjunction with the Department of Streets and other partners to establish green street design standards. Not only will this plan create some long-term jobs in the future, it will also help bring people within the community together and give them pride in the future of their neighborhoods. City workers and volunteers still have to work hard to communicate all the specifics of the project, since it involves new concepts for most people. Saliga says the organizations continue to educate people not only about the program, but also about the ways individuals can help improve the watershed on their own properties.

"The people who get involved are inspired by this type of project because they're doing things they need to do in the community. We're all able to achieve organizational goals, but we're also able to reach the goals of the water department as well. Everyone is learning, spreading the word. We're working together to make it happen," Saliga says. "It's not going to happen overnight, but it's happening, and it is really exciting. It will have an impact. We're mimicking the model of Nature to clean the water. The more projects we can do like this, the bigger impact we can have."

Dahme says it is certainly inspiring change within the communities where construction has already begun. "When people experience it and then get it, I have seen how it inspires people to help us support additional green storm-water infrastructure projects in their community, and I have even been told that it has impacted behavior like more recycling, more energy consciousness, etc. Also, a lot of our projects occur on a block scale, so many are impacted at once," Dahme says. "As a result, we have been told that it strengthens community by bringing neighbors together under one unifying project. Pretty neat that green storm-water infrastructure can impact changes in behavior and inspire a sense of community!"

Philadelphia's torch on watershed improvement has turned lots of heads. Many cities are in contact with the PWD, wanting to learn more from their innovative approach to water issues, including New York City.

"Being a part of something that provides innumerable benefits to our society on environmental, social, and economic levels into the future is tremendous. In addition, the fact that PWD is the first to take on this approach, under the circumstances, says a lot about the leaders of the city, the staff of the Philadelphia Water Department, the partners who are ambassadors of the program, and the impacted public that champions the plan," Dahme says. "In order to transform Philadelphia into a green city with clean waters, we have a lot of work ahead of us—changing policies, developing regulatory programs, creating incentives, finding funding commitments, strengthening partnerships and creating new ones, etc., while ensuring that rate-payers are on board. Being a part of a utility that leads by example and that wants to help transform the way it operates for the greater good of the city is also remarkable."

Turning T-Shirts into Trees

When we were children, we were so much more in touch with various aspects of life's unknowns because we had yet to accept the rigid parameters of adult reality. Our dreams and imaginations had so much more vigor and meaning. It's a shame we lose touch with that as we get older. However, some people never lose touch with their childhood dreams or imagination.

Imagine a little eight-year-old girl from Ohio collecting all her classmates' lunch money to help save the rain forest. The ten dollars she pulled together that day earned her a trip to the principal's office and a stern lecture. But twenty years later, that same determination has turned Beth Doane's dream into a reality. Doane's fashion company, Raintees, is saving rain forests one T-shirt at a time. For every organic T-shirt her company sells, a tree is planted in rain forests in various continents including Central America, South America, and Africa.

"I was very passionate about Nature and wildlife as a child. I told my classmates we could save the monkeys, other animals, and the rain forest," recalled Doane. "It's something I still feel very passionate about clearly."

Timber from rain-forest trees is deemed extremely valuable by logging companies and governments. Most of the destroyed rain forest is replaced with commercial crops and grazing for cattle, creating more soil erosion while annihilating precious ecosystems. It is estimated we are losing 137 plant, animal, and insect species each day due to rain forest destruction. That equates to 50,000 species each year. It is estimated that we lose more than 100 acres of rain forests each hour. Rain forests once covered more than 14 percent of the planet, but they now represent less than six percent. At the current rate of destruction, rainforests will be wiped out in less than 40 years.

People like Beth Doane are trying to prevent that through not only education and awareness, but also through daily action. Doane traveled to Central America during and after college, visiting the rain forests and the people who live in and near them.

"There are rain forests in the U.S. People don't realize it," says Doane. "There's so much that is a delicate balancing mechanism for our entire planet. The more education we can do around that the better, because once people start to realize just how crucial rain forests are it can solve a lot of other problems we're seeing now.

"Because there's been a lot more awareness, there's been more pressure on governments and some of the corporations who destroy rain forest for their profits. And, we have to be careful if we use those products. It's really looking at what we can do in general to stop depleting the rain forests because there is such a wealth of products that can come from that area. But if it's not approached sustainably, you can trash the entire ecosystem and then you have nothing. This is what they're finding with cattle ranching because when you destroy acres and acres of rain forests for meat and soybean production, it is not sustainable."

Raintees utilizes artwork by children from these countries for the designs on the front of its T-shirts. It works with children in areas where there is an excessive amount of environmental destruction. Her company also donates school supplies, asking children to draw what they see happening around them.

"The goal of our company is to show the world that we can all end environmental destruction. And it is simple. It's as simple as buying a T-shirt," says Doane. "And just show the world that it is children who are experiencing this, and it is also children who are our future, and they're the ones who are going to have to make big decisions down the line. We've been able to plant thousands of trees. Beyond that we've been able to track these children's lives. We've witnessed many inspiring stories that started very tragically but ended very positively. I think that the most incredible part of what I do is getting to see that there is hope. The power of children is so strong. One amazing story I love, out of Costa Rica . . . This little girl came up with the idea that an endangered species of monkey could be saved by taking blue rope out of her garage and stringing it between the trees, and the monkeys would use that rope to cross between trees. These monkeys were getting hit by cars, they were getting electrocuted by power lines . . . it helped save that species from [extinction]."

This little eight-year-old girl's dream was transformed into reality, allowing other children to experience the power of self-expression.

"We've also been able to find schools that didn't have art programs, and we've been able to give them art supplies for the first time or start art programs for them. Seeing a child for the first time hold a crayon and explore themselves through that crayon and their artwork—it's been an amazing experience and great to bring that to these children," says the Ohio native.

Although her design and consulting company, Andira, is doing well these days, Doane says it hasn't been easy convincing the rest of the buying public or fashion world of her ideas when the company launched in 2008.

"They didn't want to spend the extra money because it was organic, but having said that, we've done really well since then," says Doane. "To be completely honest, I think fashion is sadly going to be one of the last places where pure consciousness reigns. And I say that because it is an industry based almost completely and exclusively on 'external.' You know, how does this look, what is the brand, how much does it cost? The whole industry is based on trying to fulfill a false ideal, which is 'if you have this product, you'll become a better person,' which is completely contrary to any kind of conscious advancement as a society. That's the really tricky thing about fashion. Trying to tie fashion to consciousness is what we're trying to do and make a brand that gets people thinking, makes people more aware. It's been very interesting because you're dealing with people who are forced to think how much does it cost, will it sell, and to play to the mind of the consumer who is looking to find that thing to fulfill that life inside of them. Any kind of product or advertisement is geared to the idea that you have to feel like you need it."

Even though the fashion industry is all about appearance, Doane says she senses a change occurring in people's purchasing habits.

"The positive is that more people every day want to do good with what they purchase. They want something that they can feel proud of and also to feel that they are doing something to help," she says. "There's always a way to change things for the better. We just have to figure out what that is that we can do to help make that change. I've learned that nothing is impossible . . . that there is always a way. I've learned that educating can come in so many ways."

Doane says it is important for her to stay grounded. Even though she owns and runs an eco-friendly company, she continues to teach and practice yoga. She also makes certain to visit rain forests and the schools at least twice a year.

"I love working with the children and the people," says Doane. "I think everyone should follow their passion, follow your bliss. Life is so incredible, and we're only here for a blink of an eye, so why not live to our fullest? I can't imagine just going back to a job. I'm just a huge proponent of 'following what it is that makes you truly happy and everything else will fall into place.' If you're doing what you love, love will find you in more ways than one."

I Am Weather

I am weather
weather is me
emotion
energy
charging across the night sky
releasing
invigorating
life's continuous motion
of birth, death, and rebirth

In a roll of thunder
my voice echoes across the land
like an ancient drumbeat
my pulse connected to the Earth's heart

Like a raging river
I am uncontrollable
like drought
my thirst is never quenched
my cup never empty
my cup never full
only pouring
or waiting to be poured
into the canyon of another's being

Dream within a Dream

Waking up in middle of restless night,
rolling over to the east and hear a whispering voice
but can neither tell what the voice says nor recognize
    who it is that speaks
sheets doubled in fists, I shake with fear
not knowing who is there or what the words mean
I fall back to sleep only to hear same voice again
and tremble with greater fear
this morning, I now understand
it is the voice I've been waiting for my whole life
finally hearing the answer
but I am not ready,
am I still too afraid to accept what I'm intended to do
or admit who I am intended to be?

Son of the Lorax

I am the son of the Lorax
for I also speak for the trees
not just for me
or the bumble bee
but for all humanity
and all living things
trees are living beings
not food for machines

Trees are the lungs
they breathe for you and me
trees are not currency
not dollars and cents
that makes no sense
for all this destruction
in the name of construction
is nothing more than lunacy
has everyone gone crazy?

You see, I speak for the trees
for without their roots,
branches, limbs, and leaves
there is no more you
there is no more me
so stand up, stand up I say
help me help the trees stay

Embracing Wind

Out here
it is easy to dismiss wind
to turn my nose against your push
your persistence seems rude
constantly invading my territory
like some outraged ruler
determined to take everything from me

This is a lesson I must learn
to embrace wind
to listen to your lesson
to welcome the change
the howling transition
shaking me to the core

You are change, dear wind
change for the better
taking away what we don't need
running with the last inch of yarn
to reveal the spool's splintery marrow

Year-Long Drought

Rain has become nothing more than a ghost
a name whispered in every household
a part of every conversation
but not a part of this world
it's as if our clouds have crossed over
into another world
where we all go once we've breathed our last
in this form

Rain's aroma is never forgotten
it's like the perfume of your first lover
its breath is like the voice of your father
its sound the heartbeat of your mother
but now that the comfort is gone
it is up to us to figure out why the prolonged absence
has left such a huge void in our lives
have we forsaken ourselves
only to awaken all of our self?
only the magic of rain
can remind us of who we were meant to be

We torture ourselves with painful prognosis
and curse the inexcusable desertion
this abandonment feels unforgivable
despite its pain, we dare to search

search for the connection deep within
that last drop that hangs from our tongue
and clings to our heart like a phantom necklace
awaiting our trembling hands to open its locket

so the sacred raindrop might be released
freed from our chest
freed from our pessimism
freed from our fears

Once we conjure rain's spirit
we'll never forget the miracle that it is
and the magic it brings
to everyone
to every living thing

Pillar of Salt

A heart of lead
soon turns your soul to stone
much regret
such worries leave you standing alone
a pillar of salt
isn't worth one last look
the past is in the past
our only reality is what lies ahead

Sky crying flames
brimstone burning bridges
across waters misunderstood
and me with my umbrella
singing and dancing in rain of fire
eyes fixed firmly ahead

Rain Trance

I sit and stare into this heat wave of misunderstanding
knowing this is some sort of test of will
perhaps of character
is this our own undoing?
an unraveling of the spooled yarn?
have we traveled too far down the path of destruction?

My meditative trance hovers over the shadows
of sobbing sweat
peering through the horizon's boiled bubbles
and catches a glimpse of the other side
where there is no heat
no drought
no fear
no regret
only thoughts of rain

CHAPTER THREE

Walking a New Path
Maintaining Sustainability

More and more as we come closer and closer in touch with nature and its teachings are we able to see the Divine and are therefore fitted to interpret correctly the various languages spoken by all forms of nature about us.

GEORGE WASHINGTON CARVER

Nature's Medicine Spirit

I am Nature. Nature is me.

The connection between our own bodies and the Earth is unbreakable. Even if we try to deny this truth, evidence of it confronts us each and every moment. How we treat our own bodies is likely reflected in how we treat our surrounding environment. If we respect our own bodies, how can we not respect the Earth? They are one and the same. Likewise, if we are disrespecting our bodies with unhealthy habits, we are less likely to make a healthy connection between our bodies and the Earth.

By balancing mind, body, and spirit, not only are we enhancing our own physical well-being, but we are also building a stronger connection to all things. If we are ruled by negative emotions, like stress, anger, resentment, and regret, it is difficult to maintain higher levels of awareness. Fear and other negative emotions keep us in a constant fight-or-flight mentality, which all creatures experience when they feel threatened. But if we always feel threatened, our minds and bodies are in a state of constant mental and physical stress, exhausting us of energy that could otherwise be valuably used.

Often, much of the society we've created this past century

encourages this type of behavior in people. Fear is a key ingredient of our daily experience. Negative headlines dominate the mass media. Fear is perpetuated by political figures as a means to disguise new laws that strip away our constitutional rights and basic freedoms. Our personal intelligence is often insulted as we are treated like children by our government officials who hide truths, insisting on fear's illusion as a means of pursuing personal and clandestine agendas. Meanwhile, key industries such as agriculture and healthcare have been confiscated by corporations, erasing the potential for healthy rational thinking and the use of effective natural remedies.

We abandoned the Medicine Spirit long ago. Between the 1930s and 1980s, corporations brainwashed us away from every last healing herb or natural remedy. We stopped being healers of the emotional body and instead became mechanics of the physical body. Western medicine favored pharmaceutical prescriptions, chemotherapy, and unnecessary surgeries to heal our bodies. If something causes us pain, often the remedy is to remove it, whether it be an organ or even a limb. Scalpels and stitches have become more accepted than the power of healing hands and sacred plants. We've outcast the magic and mystique of medicine men and women, shamans, and "witch doctors" in favor of very expensive techniques incorporating surgeries, chemotherapy, radiation, long-term toxic prescriptions that induce organ failure, and other outrageous methods that weaken and unbalance the human body and spirit. Little, if any, attention is paid to our daily diet or thought processes, let alone our experiences within Nature.

According to a 2007 report by the Centre for Environment and Society at the University of Essex in England, we react much more favorably to our experiences outdoors rather than indoors. Researchers conducted an experiment with people on two different types of walks; one group walked outdoors in a park with woods and a lake, the other walked indoors in a shopping mall. The results from the experiment were staggering. After the Nature walk, 71 percent of participants felt less depressed, 71 percent less tense, 53 percent less angry, 71 percent less fatigued, and 53 percent more vigorous. But following the walk in the shopping mall, 22 percent of the participants experienced a higher depression level, 33 percent felt no change in their level of depression, and 50 percent reported feeling more tense.[1]

We have allowed the distraction of convenient products to dismantle our connections to the magic of Nature. The little pills produced by our technological progressions became our magic. Pills eclipsed plants. The pharmacist leapfrogged the alchemist. White coats and stethoscopes overrode colorful robes and herbs. Scalpels and anesthesia replaced healing hands and spiritual journeys. In this dismantling, we forgot how to be human because we tried to replace Nature with technology. Our connection to other living things was severed. Now is our chance to heal this sacred bond.

Again, how did this happen? Because we let it. We stopped listening to the wise rationality of our elders. Instead, we began listening to the advice of complete strangers to whom we have to pay money so that they will listen to us speak about our problems. We stopped walking in Nature and started sitting in offices. We bulldozed the wilderness so we could buy endless amounts of goods in shopping malls. We poisoned all the wild plants so we could plant endless acres of the same plant. We concreted the prairie to put up fast-food joints and restaurant chains. We cut down ancient trees to build houses and things we could put inside the houses to sit on or impress our guests with. We stopped listening to the wind, the river, and all the wondrous creatures so we could create more man-made diseases and more man-made cures.

We must ask ourselves: Do we want to be healed emotionally,

---

1. "Ecotherapy—The Green Agenda for Mental Health," Mind week report, May 2007, www.mind.org.uk/assets/0000/2138/ecotherapy_report.pdf, p. 2.

physically, and spiritually? Or do we merely want to mask the problem with chemical-laced pills or rid ourselves of the problem by literally cutting it out? Do we not want to know why those pains and diseases have manifested themselves inside our bodies? We must get to the root of the problem, dig deep beneath the surface, and discover why particular parts of our bodies are expressing themselves in the form of problems or pains.

Enter the wonders of Nature. Traveling down the East Coast, I spoke at the Common Good City Farm in Washington, DC, in the spring of 2010. Dozens of volunteers made it out that day to haul and shovel compost as well as till fresh earth, making room for more seeds, plants, and trees on this city block. Joining the work, I met several smiling souls enjoying the Saturday morning labor. One was a bright-eyed young lady wielding a pick axe for the first time, churning up fresh, wet earth. I asked her what she was doing.

She simply struck a pose and boldly stated, "Pick axe . . . check it!" with a bright smile from ear to ear.

We immediately became friends. She said her name was Tracey George. The more we talked, the more I could see how much of a positive impact working on the farm was having on her. Later that afternoon, she talked about how much happier and healthier she was since joining the farm.

Tracey put into words what perhaps many people feel about their own personal lives. She found herself loathing an existence unnatural to her.

"I'd gotten to the point where I didn't know why I was continuing to live life this way. The goals I had when I was much younger just didn't make any sense to me anymore," says the Cleveland, Ohio, native.

In her early twenties, Tracey had rushed through college and was working as a paralegal at a large DC law firm, where the daily grind was getting to her. The farm was an escape from a world swamped with paperwork, dim offices, deadlines, and constant stress. She said the farm was exactly the transition she needed in her life.

"It has absolutely opened a new world for me," says Tracey, who eventually joined the Peace Corps. "When Spencer, the farm manager, gave me a little tour of the farm back in February, I wasn't sure it was for me. I was excited to explore something new and do outdoorsy things, but my lack of interest in environmental studies in school concerned me. But I had to get this experience for Peace Corps, and really I had to get this experience for me. So I started volunteering there a few times a week, and I couldn't get enough."

Tracey had suffered from chronic fatigue syndrome more than a year earlier and had been diagnosed with borderline narcolepsy. But her newfound love for farm life revitalized her existence.

"I was immensely more energetic and really loved the physical work, the real tangible work that I had been craving and completely missing as a paralegal," she says. "I've always known that I'm a very physical person—physically intimate, meaning comes from touch, etc. And with some self-reflection with the farm I realized that this tangible work—shoveling woodchips and laying out warm compost with my hands rather than with a rake—perfectly lined up with what I love and what makes me feel good. The increased intake of fresh air was an improvement in itself as well.

"It's been difficult for me to find things I get truly excited about—get butterflies in my stomach, care to do over a long period of time—but this constant work at the farm has kept me engaged," said the graduate of American University.

Tracey said she had been able to spend one Saturday at the farm alone as it was closed for the day. She had talked the farm manager into letting her do some work and ended up fully embracing her relationship with Nature.

"It was wonderful. I worked in the beautiful sun, shoveling and hauling compost from one end of the farm to the other to build up this bed. I thought how surprised or disbelieving a vast majority of my friends would be, seeing me dirty and doing physical work and absolutely loving it. But it was becoming me. The first moment I got tired was the first time I sat down all morning. I realized that maybe after all these years of struggling with fatigue and a lack of interest in things (quite possibly tightly interconnected with each other), maybe this was it, or at least the start of something to bring me back to life. It's quite intense and wonderful.

"I would never have known how I truly felt about it or how my body reacted to Nature until I really engulfed myself in it. It's not an appreciation I gained from studying it in school, or hearing news stories about the environment being depleted, or seeing how much paper we waste at the firm. The only thing that could have brought me to this place of excitement and appreciation—and the thing that did bring me here—was actually doing it. Doing it. I had to do it, feel it, use my muscles, feel sore the next day, get dirt and compost under my finger nails, feel my body and muscles working on the earth . . . smell the farm and the air—and for something tangible. This engagement and transformation really could not have happened unless I was there at the farm doing the work.

"I always compared my body's state of fatigue to different types of water. Naturally, I feel like tap water, from the earth but cluttered with crap. When I've been on meds (mostly stimulants) to help fight fatigue, I feel like bottled water, clean but fake and with a plastic aftertaste," says Tracey, who is now serving in the Peace Corps. "The version I've always dreamed about being is water from a creek, pure and untouched. I fantasize about getting there, and I think Nature is the way."

Our Inner Wilderness

Wilderness is Nature untamed, unbridled. Wilderness is Nature's innate rebellion. We need wilderness as much, if not more than tamed Nature. We desire the wild. Sterilizing Nature should not be our objective . . . no more than obliterating Her.

Enriching Nature should be our main objective as humans. By allowing ourselves to reconnect we learn to listen, observe, imitate, and most importantly in this early part of the 21st century, to embrace our role as healers in Nature. This intensifies our own personal healing. We do this by giving back more than we take. Due to so many years of taking more from Nature than giving, this challenge now rests firmly on our shoulders. We cannot expect to balance this equation only on a physical level. This is impossible because we've taken so much so quickly over the past 100 years. This replenishment must also involve our emotional, mental, and spiritual energies.

If wilderness is Nature untamed, higher consciousness is Self unmolested. If Nature is Human Spirit, we can choose to either suffocate or nurture the most precious aspect of what we are as flesh-and-bone creatures, as vibrant beings. Do we allow the rivers to flow freely in our world or create stagnant waters incapable of making it to the sea? Does this not typify exactly the form of the paralysis within our own existence? We seek to manipulate Nature by constantly restricting Her from doing what she knows best—being free. If we free our own minds from the prison of this paralysis, true life flows—creating more life, more energy, more truth. Just as all things are re-energized and complete the circle or journey of life If we allow every last drop of the river to reach the sea.

This is our purpose, our journey. I truly believe we are to be Nature's guardians. In a way, we are this planet's protectors . . . if only from ourselves. Through proper rotational grazing and crop biodiversity, we encourage Nature to flourish on multiple levels, not just on one or two. One type of brush or tree may dominate the landscape if we are not managing it correctly. Here in parts of Texas and the rest of the southwestern United States, mesquite trees can dominate grassland if left unattended. In other parts of the northern U.S., it may be white pine. Proper grubbing, pruning, and thinning are needed to discourage wildfires and encourage diversity for the ecosystem.

But there is a fine line between being helpful stewards and destructive manipulators, and we can easily cross it if we do more for money than ecological balance. We might ask, for example, why one species has begun to dominate the local landscape in a particular area. Is its existence justified, but we're simply not willing to accept the reasons? Have we disrupted the natural flow or chain of command in Nature to such a point that we believe we are the only important species and that everything should be managed for our own short-term gain? Elephants, hippopotamuses, and giraffes have their proper role in the Serengeti (home of the largest mammal migration in the world), as do the 70 other large animals and 500 avifauna species. Together they maintain a balanced ecosystem that continually thrives, but we have now lost that rich diversification across most of the planet. We've either slaughtered most of the large mammals or imprisoned them in zoos. So, what is the way to balance our local ecosystems? Where do the answers lie to such a difficult question? Those answers come to us through Nature. The Earth, plants, trees, rocks, and animals are all teachers willing to enlighten or inform us of what is needed as long as we are willing to listen and learn.

Nature has a way of balancing herself through cycles. Humanity can often disrupt these cycles by interfering too much or by introducing displaced wildlife or vegetation. It is crucial that we truly examine the potential effects of our actions or reactions on Nature before we act upon an idea or theory. We must ask ourselves what is best for the ecosystem and fully understand what our methods will do to existing life in the area. To do this properly, we must get in touch with our own inner wilderness.

Dreaming is the perfect way to freely explore our own personal inner wilderness. Too often, we forget these dreams or simply pass them off as being due to an overactive imagination. I believe our dreams reveal what we are experiencing in our own personal lives but are ignoring. They can give us insight into the true meaning of our own thoughts, ideas, fears, phobias, goals, and pursuits. I find it important to write down dreams immediately when I wake up in the night. If I wait until morning, I forget the details. It is as if our mind only catches a glimpse here and there. If we blink, we might miss it.

Get in the habit of remembering your journey in the dream world. Go to bed early. Wake up at least once during the night to write down your dreams. Perhaps get up and walk around—this also keeps you from drifting too far for too long in the dream world. Our dreams are a way of taking us to another world or at least deep into our subconscious or higher consciousness. Many people keep a dream journal next to their bed. If you wait until morning, chances are you won't remember the details, if anything at all.

Building from the Earth

The way we have come to view and treat our "inner" selves has, of course, had repercussions on how we view Nature. We now find ourselves looking at Nature from the outside as if we were simply a witness to Her processes. We have become visitors to an art gallery viewing all the masterpieces on the walls without realizing that we, too, are actually another brilliant work of art on display.

For many years, homes have been nothing more than manufactured blocks spat out of a vast conveyer belt. These cookie-cutter houses are lined up in modern neighborhoods like giant tombstones in a contemporary graveyard and are now marketed and sold from sea to shining sea. No circles . . . just one square after another. Regimented living bred by a militant generation following World War II.

We should be building our homes according to our surroundings and climate. The adobe structures of eastern New Mexico have always fascinated me. They are perfect examples of a culture building houses according to its environment. Rock houses of Central Texas also intrigue me. For our house, we combined both methods using adobe and rock, blending south and west in the mixture. It is an extremely strong structure, very effective in keeping the elements on the outside. Even as temperatures dip below 40 degrees Fahrenheit, our indoor temperature stays in the low seventies. On the flip side, as summer heat hovers around 102 degrees, we're comfortable inside at about 72 degrees.

It is imperative that our houses and other structures become extensions of the local landscape—not manufactured blocks from materials often shipped from hundreds or even thousands of miles away. Construction should focus on using local resources as well as concepts that are environmentally and energy friendly. Buildings should be constructed of local materials, employing methods that keep the structure strong and energy efficient. Rock, earth, straw, mud, bamboo, and hemp are at the top of those lists. Long-time "Earthship" house constructor and designer Michael Reynolds has used "junk" to build beautiful homes in the Taos, New Mexico, area for more than 30 years now. Reynolds utilizes everything from old car tires and beer bottles to mud and straw as building blocks for the outer walls.

One day, when my oldest son was four years old, we had a conversation about our house. He asked, "What's this house's name?"

I responded, "I don't know. What do you think this house's name should be?"

His eyes peering toward the heavens, he tapped his forefinger to his cheek in deep thought and said, "I think its name is Selah."

I had him repeat the name over and over because I'd never heard this word before. Sure enough, he spelled it with an "s" and enunciated the word carefully. I asked him several times if he was saying Sara. Emphatically, he shook his head and said, "No!" over and over.

"Selah?" I reaffirmed. "You're sure?"

"Selah! That's what I said!"

Quickly I typed *Selah* into the computer. To my astonishment, I discovered it was the Hebrew word for "rock." The word also means a break in a song, a pause. Staring into the smiling face of my son, I was speechless. How did he know this word? I asked teachers, my wife, and the rest of the family. No one else had said this word to him before. Nobody else had even heard it. I knew my son was not really a genius, but a real genuine soul in touch with things far beyond our grasp because he was still in tune with all the magical energies and sacred languages of the Earth.

Altering Our Thoughts on Energy

It is quite comical to think of all the panic put into our heads by news stories of "energy shortages" or "energy crises" or any other potential failure humanity will have to endure in the near future. Will our lives change because of more expensive oil? Absolutely. But, if we cave in to the fearmongering police who dictate what we can or cannot do, we limit our potential and give in to their limited thinking. We must operate outside the realms of current potentiality and expectation. We must break new ground and not settle for the norm.

Dr. Kevin Mulligan of Texas Tech University has taken an in-depth look at the development of wind energy and other renewable energy in West Texas. Usually, renewable energy is associated with environmentally friendly policies.

"I don't think people see what's coming. We mapped six to seven thousand wind turbines just off the Llano," says Dr. Mulligan. "What scares me is what life will be like on the High Plains, living among 20 or 30 thousand wind turbines. That scares the hell out of me. When you get into the tens of thousands of wind turbines, the whole landscape becomes very industrial. Substations and power lines. You're seeing that in Sweetwater, Texas, right now. It's not just the turbines, it's the electrical grid. The landscape is becoming basically industrialized. It's a new landscape. We think of industrial landscapes being factories and rural landscapes being farms, but when you get thousands of turbines, you get a combination of the two."

Mulligan is insistent that industrialized wind energy can't sustain itself any more than the continual mining of the water of the Ogallala.

"The whole wind industry is nonsensical to me. It just can't support itself, so it lives on a political whim. This is another example of our government setting us up for failure by creating another bubble set up to burst," says Mulligan.

He reiterated that this is a pattern we've seen repeated throughout history, comparing resource exploitation to colonization.

"Isn't this the definition of a colony? The area being colonized is exporting resources and getting very little in return," says the Texas Tech professor of geography. "I look at this area. Where is all of this electricity going? We're the colonies here, our resources are getting extracted . . . our water, electricity. We get all the crap, and we don't get a lot in return. The thing that concerns me about the wind energy is that you get a whole lot of money for the wind turbines, but what happens when you get Wall Street investors coming in and buying the property? When it's gone, it's gone, and that's sort of been our history of natural resources extraction."

While mega-watt wind turbines may not be the ideal solution to some, wind energy continues to grow worldwide. Over the past decade, wind energy has grown from 20 to 40 percent each year. In 2000, only 17,400 MW (megawatts) of wind energy were generated worldwide. By 2005, that had jumped to 59,091 MW. In 2010, wind industry production continued to surge, reaching 168,828 MW despite economic struggles in the U.S. Current trends will likely double that production by 2013 and triple it by 2016.

Energy production is no different than food production or economics—for it to be efficient and sustainable it must be localized. More focus needs to be placed on smaller systems to sustain individual houses or communities rather than large-scale systems exporting energy from America's heartland to the large urban areas of the Northeast. It is also imperative we combine multiple forms and sources of alternative energies so we are not creating a monopoly of energy sources in one area.

Solar power continues to grow at a rate of 20 to 25 percent each year. Prices for solar power equipment are slowly dropping, making it more appealing to individuals and communities. Despite this, most families are not going to spend $10,000–$15,000 on solar power installations for their homes. Until small-scale renewable energy installations become more affordable, the industrialized versions will continue to dominate the landscape.

More of us must learn to implement these systems and to construct energy systems, whether they be solar or wind. Solar makes sense since the sun comes up every single day, no matter what. In some places, though, like the Pacific Northwest, Alaska, and even the Northeast, there are many days when clouds dissipate the sun's strength. However, across the American southwest, solar should excel.

Wind also makes a lot of sense in areas where wind forces are consistent. Often there are obstacles to overcome, though, such as tall buildings, hills, and trees. This is why West Texas and the Midwest have seen so much wind turbine construction in the past ten to fifteen years—there are very few obstructions.

One of the most promising systems already working in this country is landfill energy. This is a system devised to harness the methane gas released from the huge mounds of waste in landfills and convert it into energy usable in power plants, manufacturing facilities, vehicles, homes, and businesses. As of 2011, there were 558 operational landfill energy projects in the country and another 510 candidate sites.

Sustainability advocate, consultant, and speaker Jake Stewart helped to implement the landfill energy project in Denton, Texas. He said it is an incredibly easy process and is economically feasible for urban areas.

"There's an argument we shouldn't be putting energy into the landfill to begin with. That's a separate argument," says Stewart. "But we've got a heck of a lot of landfills with lots of organic matter cooking right now. I'm a big fan of literally drilling wells into these landfills and taking out that gas. There is some engineering involved and it is a strategic process, but there is a lot of potential in that."

Stewart's landfill energy project harnessed the landfill gas and powered an energy system for biodiesel production employing used cooking oil. He says the Denton area produces more than 20 million gallons of cooking oil grease. The methane gas was used to heat the boilers, which helped power the biodiesel production process. The biodiesel was then used to help power much of the city's fleet of working vehicles.

Stewart has started a few different companies in the past 13 years. He's focused on renewable energy on a local level, helping establish systems in rural areas of Africa and Mexico. He said water treatment facilities also have a lot of potential, as all forms of waste can be a solution.

Bringing a scientific mind to the table, Stewart has been able to address problems in many projects over the years. But he says that often there are some misconceptions about renewable energy and cautions people to not write off one type of renewable energy simply because of propaganda and misunderstandings.

"If I'm making ethanol from waste products, taking woody biomass and making cellulosic ethanol from a process that's not using a crop such as corn, then it's a much different scenario. Now, you're talking about an energy balance that's positive . . . Corn-based ethanol doesn't make a bit of damn sense, but taking leftover stalks from sugarcane that [are] piled up and burned . . . using that makes a lot of sense."

Stewart also points out that companies like ExxonMobil spend millions to protect the future of fossil-fuel energy by spreading propaganda against green energy and climate change issues. He says they took a page out of the tobacco industry's book by deciding that they don't need to win the argument against biofuels and climate change—it's enough simply to keep it going.

Much like farming, it is important that our future energy sources are not monopolized. And it is just as crucial that our future energy sources be diverse.

"True energy security is just like investing. You don't want all your eggs in one basket," says Stewart. "Localization has benefits on multiple fronts . . . [You] get that localized involvement out of a necessity rather than writing your congressman. There's too much distance in that to actually carry the level of impact for what we eat. But when you're talking about a city council–level petition, you've got a degree of impact and involvement that is chewable. You can actually see it into fruition."

Stewart says one individual and fifty friends can make a huge impact on the local level, while at the state and national levels, they would encounter a greater degree of difficulty because of the big-money interest groups they'd run into.

"That's where that empowerment starts to be appealing. You're not going toe-to-toe with ExxonMobil," says Stewart.

No matter the form of renewable energy, we must evaluate the full scope of the process. We have to ask and answer several questions to ensure it is the best energy system we can implement. As oil prices rise, we'll be forced to ask tougher questions and make more difficult decisions about our daily lifestyles.

"What is the carbon balance?" asks Stewart. "We really need to get a positive energy equation. What's the cost we're not looking at with fossil-fuel production? Are we looking at all the hidden costs of environmental and health problems? You can make a really strong argument for renewables if you talk about the hidden costs. Nobody wants to talk about the hidden costs of oil and coal. They just want to say it's cheaper."

Few people realize that fossil-fuel production by these billion-dollar corporations is heavily subsidized. Much like our food system, subsidies are a huge part of the reason the U.S. has relatively cheap energy costs in comparison to most countries. We pay less at the pump thanks to subsidies. Those very subsidies continue to allow fossil fuels to be a more economical choice over renewable energies.

"People don't want to subsidize renewable energy. I say great. Let's not subsidize it. But let's take away the tax breaks and artificial subsidization of fossil fuels. Let's level the playing field," says Stewart. "Ten times out of ten the renewables will win. A lot of the conservative argument is let's let the free market do it. Great, let's create a free market and remove the billions of dollars of subsidies going to the fossil-fuel industry and let's play ball."

It is important that we don't fall for the scam of large-scale corn ethanol production plants or any other industrialized form of renewable energy. That is a bubble set up to burst because without heavy subsidies, these multi-hundred-million-gallon plants cannot sustain themselves. We need local energy that doesn't have to be subsidized by government in order to function. We need to focus on biodiesel production of certain nonfood crops, so we are not sacrificing food for fuel. There isn't enough farmable land to satisfy all our current needs for biofuels and food. Who wants to starve to death while driving a gas-guzzling machine to nowhere? We can realistically supplement only a fraction (less than 10 percent) of our modern fuel needs with biodiesel and still produce food crops to feed seven billion and growing. That means we also need to be curtailing our fossil-fuel usage as individuals and as a society.

Foundation of Ecovillages and Transition Towns

As we evolved in the 20th century, our principles for constructing and expanding towns and cities continued to steer us away from a true community-living concept. As corporate consumerism ruled our lives, especially following World War II, cities stretched upward and outward to fuel the fires of perpetual growth. These strategies have begun to fail in the early part of the 21st century. Whether we look at economics, government, or employment figures, our country is slipping from its place atop the pyramid—a position we have worked feverishly to achieve and have boasted about to the rest of the world.

In contrast to this sprawl of shopping centers and subdivisions are the models of ecovillages and transition towns popping up here and there across the country. These models involve a simple philosophy to ensure the prosperity not only of towns and villages, but also the people. Transition towns (or transition networks/movements) are a grassroots community effort to transition existing cities, towns, neighborhoods, and so on into a new paradigm that addresses vital issues such as peak oil, climate change, and economic instability. Ecovillages are communities designed to be more sustainable in three major ways: socially, economically, and ecologically.

Author and activist Albert Bates began working on the Ecovillage Training Center in 1994. He was the perfect candidate since he's been living in an ecovillage in Tennessee since 1972. He says ecovillages or transition towns can be established anywhere from downtown Los Angeles to rural areas in third-world countries.

"Ultimately, they all have the same kind of goal, which is to create a human avocation that is sustainable into future generations," says Bates. "The three-legged stool model. One leg is ecological, keeping it in harmony with Nature. Second is social, in the aspect of how people relate to each other and the planet. Really that gets into what are your ethics, shared vision of the world, and your mission in life. The third leg is the financial/economic sustainability. If it's not financially stable, it's not going to be there very long, no matter how much fun it is. When you get all three legs stable, your stool does not wobble. It's steady and each thing reinforces the other. It's a virtual cycle of improvement out into the future."

Improving the future means altering the present. How do we relay the importance of purchasing better products that cost more when we've encouraged society to consume the cheapest product on the shelf?

"You have to look at the whole life cycle of an object and ask, 'What did it really take to produce this?' Is it something that is coming from a nonrenewable source or is it something coming off the sweat of some abused person in some other part of the world?" asks Bates. "Or is it something which is an object of pride for its creator which renews and regenerates the planet. The problem is we have an economic paradigm that really looks at things in terms of GDP rather than the ability to produce well-being in the recipient and to sustain the source. That's a bad economic model that has to change."

Bates says he was hopeful that the Occupy Wall Street movement was helping us boycott various economic corruptions in this country.

"You try to minimize sourcing stuff that you know is damaging the planet or is from companies that have abusive relations with the people producing it. As you do, you find there are some ways to localize your economy. Those are things like trade-and-barter systems, farmers markets, food co-ops, CSAs, complementary currencies, or buying credits, which allow the money to stay in the area rather than going into banks or big-box stores that take it and send it off to some distant place," he says. "You can cycle money out of an area just as easily as you can cycle it in, so you really want to keep your money where you live. If you lose it, and it goes out to some rich fat cat sitting in some skyscraper in a distant city, that's not helping your community anymore. That money is gone."

Having taken an active part in introducing this concept through public speaking and seminars, Bates says the ecovillage lifestyle is also a lot of fun for the community involved because the structure encourages interaction among neighbors.

"You create relationships, create friends. You have local exchanges, local finance, and infrastructure for that," says the author of The Biochar Solution. "It's fun. People find as they get together, sharing music, sharing poetry on Saturday night, it begins to pick up momentum. It's a de-cocooning phase. We had gone into this increasingly alienated society ever since the 1950s, after the television was introduced into the home. There's a whole lot of fun being missed out [on] in life if you don't get together with your family and friends to do things with."

Tens of thousands of transition towns and tens of thousands of ecovillages are in existence throughout the world. Ecovillages are more prevalent in India and South America. Bates says the higher the level of industrialization, the lower the number of ecovillages there are in a country, but many other reasons also contribute to why the U.S. is slower to adopt such philosophies.

"A lot of it has to do with our education and our diet. We're so bought into popular culture . . . and pop culture has one central story that it is telling—and it doesn't tell a story that is conducive to making large shifts of cultural change. Really the only thing that makes those kinds of shifts happen for people like us is something that disrupts the story . . . and that might be something like peak oil or climate change," he says. "Two-thirds of the world doesn't have a central story, but they do know they have certain needs. The biggest deficit that we have in the industrial world is that we've lost that sharing attitude which you find so much in the poorer parts of the world."

Bates is adamant that society must change sooner rather than later—before our destructive methods pass a point of no return from both an economical and environmental standpoint.

"This paradigm of industrial growth and the whole capitalist model where you invest toward the future expecting a dividend of return that's greater than your investment . . . that's going to have to change. We have to get to a steady-state economics model that doesn't require growth. The growth model is like a cancer. It's really the only thing in Nature that has unlimited growth, and it kills the host. And that's essentially what we're doing, we're killing Gaia, we're killing the host by expecting exponential growth, whether it's the Ogallala Aquifer or the industrialization of small towns, thinking it can be infinite. It can't."

Key Vocations for a Thriving Sustainable Community

Farmer/Gardener	Carpenter/Construction
Chef/Cook	Blacksmith/Welder
Beekeeper	Engineer
Seamstress	Electrician
Healer/Massage Therapist	Leather Maker
Ex-military/Law Enforcement	Candle Maker
Gunsmith	Plumber
Herbalist/Alchemist	Mechanic
Writer/Historian	Doctor
Tracker/Woodsman	Animal Husbandry

(There are others, but this is a nice start.)

The Sax-Appeal of Alamance County

Along the winding curves of North Carolina back roads, one finds old tobacco farms transformed into an endless line of healthy farms and homes. It's like an art gallery of farms posing in their natural beauty, smiling a warm and friendly southern smile. Each homestead has its own style and palette of colors—not a carbon copy of manufactured life and living, but rather a personal expression of human nature's independence embracing the wonders of Nature.

Nestled in the tree-filled hills on the Haw River, these homes are part of a small old mill town called Saxapahaw. The first mill was built there in 1844 but was later demolished for the cotton mill that still stands there today. This old town has almost vanished on more than one occasion. In fact, not long ago most of the current establishments were decaying, derelict buildings, but now the structures light up like old folks in a retirement home as younger generations stroll through the doors. The infusion of youth, pride, and energy gives the once-abandoned buildings a proud glow.

"Saxapahaw was much quieter than it is now," laughs Mac Jordan, the heir to Saxapahaw's redefined path to sustainability. "It's always been a real attractive place for neighbors and families to live and get to know each other, but it started to transform from a mill village of people that had grown up here because their families worked in the mill. We started marketing the houses to outsiders because my dad saw Saxapahaw being a unique alternative to your typical apartment complex or subdivision. My dad, being practical minded, said we can offer a much more self-sufficient and sustainable model for people to live."

Jordan's family has a long history of not only living in Saxapahaw, but also rescuing the small town from obscurity. In 1927, Mac's grandfather and great-uncle bought the textile mill and houses that were slowly decaying after the factory closed its doors in 1924. The Jordans kept the mill and town alive into the 1970s before selling the family business to a larger milling company. Many of the mill houses were again abandoned and becoming derelict by 1978. After years of watching the houses go to waste, Mac's father, John, decided to buy back the houses.

"This was not just about saving a community but creating an alternative to the subdivision model that was mainstream," says Mac. "We were simply trying to create a better path for the future. Communities need to start taking more responsibility for their own lives and not wait for somebody else to do it for them. We need to work more together as neighbors. That's been the model I've been following because it makes better sense than the mainstream model, which has been the opposite trend."

John Jordan and his son began to repair the old mill houses, encouraging families and individuals to move back to the rural community. The mill houses were updated to be energy-efficient with insulation and equipped with both wood-burning and natural-gas heating systems. They weren't an easy sell early on, but Mac kept his father's dream alive throughout the 1980s and 1990s. Slowly, more people were attracted to Saxapahaw. Following the philosophies of his father and grandfather, Jordan says the transition to a more sustainable village-style community is just common sense, copying a pattern that not long ago was common in this country.

"Never really thought of it as radical culture, I just thought it was practical. It's really traditional in a lot of ways in relation to community and living. We're kinda going back to the model we had two or three generations ago where communities were more self-sufficient and more cooperative, people did more things for each other more locally. We didn't have this disconnect with everything. From the sixties and seventies on, the trend has been more segregation, disconnection, and isolation of people from their environment, their community, their governments, their economies. So we all believed in a more sustainable, diverse, self-sufficient village-type of model versus what we see all around, which is more of a subdivision model where everything is separate and spread out—where you have to get in a car to drive to everything."

At the heart of the town is the old cotton mill, which is now a modernized complex of studio apartments and condos for individuals and families. Right next door is the Saxapahaw General Store, a market place that boasts a "five-star gas station." Inside, people can enjoy gourmet meals instead of the greasy grub usually found inside gas-station convenient stores. Having opened its doors in 2008, the store offers a wide range of healthy snacks and many locally grown or handmade treats.

Upstairs from the store is the Haw River Ballroom, which hosts all types of events. Last but not least is the Eddy Pub, the locals' favorite hangout. The community and visitors gather there for drinks. You won't find your typical Budweiser and Coors Light selections. The Eddy holds true to the town's mission of supporting local businesses, including breweries. On any given night, one might run into Charlie, a neuro-ophthalmologist, and cattle rancher, Dr. Jack, who designs and builds electric cars, or electric-car-owner Chris, who installs wind and solar energy systems. The downtown area has truly breathed new life back into the area.

"It has attracted more like-minded individuals because it's not really found anywhere else," says Mac. "People have really started to become more and more interested to become a part of this movement and community. There is certainly a lot we want to see expanded and developed as far as services go, but what we really want is to be true to this model of locally grown, locally made, locally owned philosophy. That way people are connected to where their food is grown, who is cooking it—so we want to see more of that."

One of those like-minded individuals drawn to Saxapahaw is Eric Henry. Henry grew up down the road from Saxapahaw and has lived in Alamance County for over 50 years. He started a T-shirt business while attending the University of North Carolina at Chapel Hill. In his senior year, he left school to help Tom Sineath start TS Designs, a T-shirt company in his hometown of Burlington, located 12 miles from Saxapahaw. "It's been a roller coaster ever since," says Henry.

The manufacturing business underwent an extremely challenging period in the 1990s after NAFTA took much of the country by storm. Most businesses closed their doors in the U.S. and shipped their jobs south of the border for cheaper labor and production costs. TS Designs took the opposite approach. The company stepped out on a long limb and invested hundreds of thousands of dollars in trying to find a more environmentally friendly dyeing process for their T-shirts. They were successful and have three patents on the innovative process. They came up with what they call a triple-bottom-line business—"People, Planet, Profits."

"Sustainability is a journey, not a destination," says Henry. "I will probably leave this planet taking more than I give back, but hopefully what we can do is find a model that can equalize that in the next generation or two."

This transition was not an easy one and was met with great hesitation in their community.

"People thought we were fruitcakes, that we should've sold out while we could," says Henry. "We were essentially swimming upstream. It was an extremely hard uphill battle because we charged higher prices for our product. We spent a lot of time explaining to our customers why we had to charge more.

"We had to start seeking out companies that had the same vision as us, like Greenpeace, Whole Foods, Ben & Jerry's Ice Cream, and a few others," said Henry. "We struggled for a lot of years. There was [a] time when we talked about bankruptcy. But there was a gut feeling that this was the right way to go through it. We just thought eventually people would start getting it, and they finally did."

The turnaround came in 2008, and they both agree that the struggle had been worth enduring to give birth to the success they have now.

"Profits are important. We just don't believe that profits are the only thing a company should be responsible for," says Henry. "We've been here for 30 years. We're still in a business they declared dead back in the 1990s. We're proving you can still have a business that has a soul and a responsibility beyond a bottom line.

"There is an opportunity for us to move forward in the future with the challenges we have in depletion of natural resources and climate change . . . we just can't do it the way we used to," explains Henry. "We want to be more efficient, more productive but not lose focus on our values. We're not going to trade off [reducing] our environmental impact . . . just to save money."

Henry and Sineath do everything they can to focus on the positive impacts their business has on their local economy. "I think there's a lot of hope at the local level. I'm very concerned with what's happening at the national level in what we're leaving for the next generation," Henry says.

The company is acting on these concerns on every possible front. More than 50 percent of the T-shirts they produce are made with North Carolina cotton. Their Cotton of the Carolinas project was launched in 2008. Cotton never leaves the state from seed to shirt. But TS Designs is more than just a T-shirt company. It is a classic model of businesses for the present and near future. The business operates on solar and wind energy, and produces and sells biodiesel as well. They also promote healthy eating by growing a full garden complete with chickens and honeybees on their property. Employees are expected to work in this garden a couple hours each week. Henry says creating a healthier working environment is beneficial on so many levels.

"I get asked a lot of times, 'What do a garden, bees, and chickens have to do with making and selling T-shirts?' *Everything*," emphasizes Henry. "I believe part of running a triple-bottom-line business is looking beyond the bottom line. Having a garden and connecting your employees to local, healthy food is a critical part of our triple-bottom-line business. I have also found it is a small tool to compete with against the giant industrial agriculture system that brought us fast food . . . and we know what fast food has done to our waist line and health. When veggies are in season we have a weekly lunch in which the employees volunteer to make a dish using veggies from the garden. We are just finishing our third season of having a company garden, and there is no question that it has helped improve our eating habits beyond McDonald's, Burger King, and KFC."

Henry admits there was a period of time where he and his wife were extremely frustrated with the community's mentality as more businesses went under in favor of a commercialized lifestyle. They decided to change that on every level possible. The Henrys and others continue to stoke the "sustainable" fires in and around Alamance County. In the spring of 2011, Company Shops Market opened its doors in downtown Burlington, introducing a locally owned cooperative grocery store that allows more people to enjoy and support the production of locally grown healthy foods. It's another example of reinvigorating a small town with local commerce.

"Burlington, like a lot of downtowns, has been devastated by the commerce of strip malls and shopping centers. What was a lively, exciting place growing up had turned into 'Deadville.' Everyone was doing their shopping somewhere else," says Henry. "We were determined to make a co-op, a business owned by the community. Another thing that is wrong with the business world is [that] the power is concentrated to a small group of people. We don't want that. We want a store that's owned by us, the money stays with us to support us."

Taking several years to get off the ground, this was a $2.6 million project for Burlington. Henry said there are over 300 cooperative grocery stores in the country and another 300 or more in planning stages. This provided the group with plenty of resources and support to keep the market's dream alive. Company Shops Market now has over 2,200 owners. The owners essentially buy stock in the company, ranging from $100 per share for individuals to $150 for families. Each share owner is eligible to be on the board of directors, and no matter how many shares each person owns, share owners have only one vote each, creating a balance of power.

"With all these things we did, it goes against everything they teach you in business school," laughs Henry. "Everyone's equal here. Nobody's more important or different than the other. We hope, as we go down the road, we need to do other businesses this way. It really vests you in your community. The response has been overwhelming. We have so many things to offer so many people. We want to make money to keep going, but we want to do a lot more than make money. Even in these tough economic times, we're gaining strength and momentum. We're doing things here. I'm very happy with the direction our community is going."

Henry and his wife have since purchased a small farm between Burlington and Saxapahaw, bridging the gap between the two communities and their involvement in both efforts to create a more efficient model of living. Mac Jordan is glad to have them and others who share the same beliefs and dream.

"The demographics of the community became much more diverse, but the life and mission of Saxapahaw of being a true village has always been its foundation and its basis. That's what we want to maintain for its future," says Mac. "This has been a very difficult pursuit because of our location and small population . . . to get enough volume to sustain small businesses, because we're not an urban location. But that's also what makes it so pristine and attractive to live here. The businesses not only need to serve the community, but they have to serve visitors to make this model successful."

Education by Nature

As more towns and communities gradually restructure their model, it is imperative that schools adopt more Nature friendly curriculums to enhance the learning environment for children. Most universities offer environmental or agriculture programs. Even the majority of high schools in the nation have some kind of agriculture class to educate young minds. But not enough time and energy is focused on the details of essential, real-life skills involving Mother Nature, as well as our kindred connection to various forms of life breathing all around us.

Yes, there are Boy Scouts, Girl Scouts, Cub Scouts, and other organizations where kids learn survival and nature skills, but only a small percentage of kids join these clubs. Yes, it is up to the parents or grandparents to help instill gardening skills such as how to germinate seeds, save seeds, and take care of various food crops, but how many parents now possess these skills? Thirty or forty years ago, most Americans were linked closely to the farm in one way or another, but we've become so far removed from the farm that many skills that were once a way of life and living have quickly vanished in a couple of generations. We need to get them back . . . and fast.

It's vital that younger generations be aware of their surroundings. With so many environmental issues facing our world today, we need young people who are aware of those problems, so that they'll be inspired to help change our world for the better. Covering their eyes and ears to those drastic issues won't make them go away.

"Getting children into Nature is such a fundamental aspect of growing up with an understanding of how our decisions can have such a large impact—locally, nationally, and even globally," says Eva Hernandez, a staff member of the Sierra Club. "It's really incredible to see how children transform and grow when you get them out of a classroom setting and teach them real-world lessons in the natural environment. Growing up with that understanding is essential for the next generation to become stewards of the environment, to ensure that our most precious places are valued and intact for generations to come."

There are close to 300 farm-based education programs across the U.S. Massachusetts alone boasts 48 programs that are FBEA (Farm-Based Education Association) members. Shelburne Farms in Shelburne, Vermont, is a classic model for other farm-education programs to follow. With 1,400 acres on the shores of Lake Champlain, they "practice rural land uses that are environmentally, economically and culturally sustainable." Created in 1886 by William Seward and Lila Vanderbilt Webb as an agriculture model, the farm is a national historic landmark that educates adults and children in healthier agriculture methods from forestry and crop production to dairy and livestock care.

According to Bill Kunze, Pennsylvania state director for the Nature Conservancy, "there's a strong correlation to whether people have Nature experiences as they grow up and whether, as adults, they will be concerned about policies that affect Nature." As we are continually faced with economic issues in this country, it's sad that environmental issues take a far backseat. As a society, we continue to raise children to focus more on money than our environment. Our focus must shift to the realities of the world of which we are a part, not the illusions that have no true meaning in the grand scheme of our existence.

As I write these words now, my five-year-old is outside playing. He prefers the outdoor environment. I started taking him on walks and eventually jogs or runs when he was only an infant. His crying fits would almost always subside the moment we stepped outside. Once I finish this book, I can't wait to spend more time doing the same with him. But even though farm work and writing often consume me, reliving my childhood with my own children remains a part of my adult existence. On second thought, I can finish this chapter later . . .

And I'm back. Surveying the landscape around our home, I asked my son which tree is his favorite. He grinned and ran to and touched a red oak I planted two years ago, shouting, "This one!" And then he proceeded to run and touch every tree on our homestead, saying they too were his favorites. It's a challenge to teach him that not every area is a playground on a farm, making sure he is safe around larger animals and in certain areas not made for horseplay. His connection with Nature is innate, though, and he reminds me never to lose touch of that part of my inner child, no matter how old I get.

While it is our duty to maintain Nature, it is also our duty to make certain that wilderness is able to survive our excessive pruning habits. Marysol Valle of Urban Roots Farm says she witnesses a transformation in young people as they participate in programs teaching basic skills such as cooking, gardening, and seed saving.

"They come out to the farm in the beginning of the program full of attitude and defense mechanisms," says Valle. "We as a staff work so hard to create a safe space for them to drop their walls and still be respected by us and their peers. They crave that safe space, and as soon as they become comfortable, we all become a big family. Not only do they learn the value of hard work, they learn the value of who they are. They learn that all things are valuable and need to be respected and loved."

Valle says the kids also learn to speak in public and learn they have the power to change the food system for the better. Although most people come into the programs completely out of touch with farm life, they leave with a better idea of how Nature functions.

"People come out to the farm, volunteers and our youth, with crazy expectations. I hear 'there has to be a faster way to do this' a lot. We live in a world where food is instant, and that is what most people expect farming to be as well," says the Austin native. "Insects freak people out, and I have to explain how valuable they are and how we wouldn't have food to eat if it wasn't for them. They are also freaked out by the weather—heat, rain, cold—they just aren't used to climate extremes, to being exposed to the outdoors. Farmville on Facebook is the closest thing to being on a farm most of them have experienced. They have unrealistic expectations when the only farming they have seen is completely fake and contrived in a video game.

"Sometimes they think that I am crazy, but I like to think I plant a seed inside every single person that comes out to the farm. One day some of those seeds will germinate, and some will even make it to fruition," states Valle. "Generally, the people that come out to the farm are the exception. Most people don't care about where their food comes from, and that is what is scary. We all eat, but only a small few are willing to take a look at how it is grown. All I can do is just keep planting seeds, in the dirt and in the people, and hope for a day when the fears of our own Nature are overcome by the realization that those fears are destroying our very existence."

As parents and grandparents, it is up to us to help nurture and encourage our children's relationship with Nature. Our own knowledge and experiences can help in this area. Many adults may not feel they are qualified to do so. This is nonsense. We're all a part of Nature, we simply have to connect ourselves to Nature. Nature Explore is a collaborative program of the Arbor Day Foundation and Dimensions Educational Research Foundation. They provide training for adults, including parents, to help provide a healthy outdoor learning environment. They provide a free Family's Club kit on their website—www.arborday.org—to get families started exploring the outdoors together. The Family Club also provides a calendar outlining suggested lesson plans:

1. Get to Know a Tree
2. Leaf Shape Adventure
3. Your Very Own Story
4. Your Special Path
5. Animal Signs
6. Texture Adventure
7. What Can You See in a Cloud?
8. What Is Beautiful to You?
9. Colors in the World

These are topics that allow children's imagination to thrive. Tina Reeble serves as an education specialist for Nature Explore in Lincoln, Nebraska. She's helped take part in research since 1998 involving children in a natural learning environment and said there is a growing movement toward families and schools educating children more through Nature.

"There's definitely a value in just being outside. What we're saying is, if you are a little bit more intentional about it, there's a learning potential for children that's incredible, that takes place outside, that just doesn't happen indoors—so take advantage of it," says Reeble. "Help children rise and be their best selves and meet the potential of who they can be as human beings. And we really can't do that if we're not connected with Nature."

Nature in Public Schools

With classrooms teasing children with a mere glimpse of Nature through a window, it's no wonder that there are children who can't focus on the material and spend their time staring out that window, daydreaming. The solution many schools provided was to eliminate windows in classrooms. Many schools have constructed lavish new buildings in the past twenty years. Sadly, most of these buildings have no view of the outdoors for children to even see what Nature looks like until recess, lunch, or the final bell affords them a quick breath in the open air before the bus ride home to their computer games. That's an even crueler existence for a child to endure daily. It's cutting off a significant portion of their existence.

Driving through various parts of New York City, I have seen children exit the front door of elementary schools with nothing but a sidewalk and a motel-room-sized playground outside. The schools were all building and no Nature. Particularly for urban schools, these children need more time in Nature to express themselves and explore the wonders of life.

America's public school system is nationalized across 50 states, spans over 3,000 miles, and serves more than 80 million students. Our children's education is replicated and mass produced like shoelaces, cardboard boxes, and chewing gum. Teachers are seldom given the freedom to stray from the state-issued curriculum. They have a tough enough job as it is, and the prisonlike classroom environment makes their task even more difficult. Students are prevented from exploring their own personal creativity by thinking outside of the box. We encourage a sanitized, sterile system that breeds obedient corporate employees, mimicking the treatment of new recruits by our armed forces.

These windowless views in the classroom are premeditative training for the corporate world. The curriculum of memorization preps them to be subservient citizens who will never question authority or disobey their teachers or corporate bosses. The public school system trains our children to accept a maze of cubicles and fluorescent lighting where they'll find comfort beside the token plant strategically placed next to the company water cooler and coffee pot.

Standardized testing dominates public schools like a phantom

144

bully, pummeling art and music programs across the country. We beat our children into submission with a stack of generic textbooks, forcing them to read opinionated versions of our species' journey through millennia. Particularly in history, these books present one side of the story and are often sugar coated and laced with falsehoods and inaccuracies. Do we really still give Christopher Columbus credit for discovering America? We have much more accurate information now. I mean, even instant replay helps officials right their wrong calls in sporting events. Is our historical ego too big to allow us to make a few corrections? And can we please admit we were the real savages during the Indian Wars of 1540 to the 1890s? A little honesty might be good therapy for all of us. Let's learn from history so we don't continue to repeat its malfeasance.

We close children up inside windowless classrooms that resemble prison cells decorated with desks and a chalkboard. Even prisoners are allowed one hour outdoors. Is PE (physical education) or recess meant to meet the minimal requirements of sunlight and exercise during a seven- to eight-hour school day? We need to encourage more imagination and creativity, rather than stifling young people's minds by coercing them into learning only reading, writing, math, and science skills. While those subjects are certainly important, they focus on one half of the brain. To fully develop not only minds, but also bodies, we need to allow children to connect with Nature so they may excel on multiple levels—not just those associated with state-required measuring sticks in the form of written exams.

In *Last Child in the Woods*, best-selling author Richard Louv writes, "An environment-based education movement—at all levels of education—will help students realize that school isn't supposed to be a polite form of incarceration, but a portal to the wider world." [2] He continues later in the award-winning book, "Passion does not arrive on videotape or on a CD; passion is

---

2. Richard Louv, *Last Child in the Woods: Saving Our Children from Nature-Deficit Disorder* (Chapel Hill, NC: Algonquin Books, 2008), p. 226.

personal. Passion is lifted from the earth itself by the muddy hands of the young, it travels along grass-stained sleeves to the heart. If we are going to save environmentalism and the environment, we must also save an endangered indicator species: the child in nature."[3]

Louv coined the term "nature-deficit disorder" and has written extensively on the natural healing wonders of Nature in our lives. The journalist serves as the founding chairman of the Children & Nature Network. It is an organization designed to help connect today's children and future generations of children to Nature.

What about children who will never enroll in Nature programs away from their schools? How do we bring Nature to these children? By teaching them when they are very young. By getting into the school system and instilling a curriculum focusing on Nature, wilderness, gardening, water filtration, seed saving, food-storage techniques, livestock husbandry, geology, entomology, botany, and countless other subjects and skills that everyone can use in order to take care of themselves and their families in the future. What good does it do us if we have an entire generation that can operate the latest and greatest iPhone, iPod, iPad, iRobot, or whatever but doesn't know where an egg comes from or doesn't know an ear of corn from an aardvark's nostril?

ADHD (attention deficit hyperactivity disorder) or ADD (attention deficit disorder) is affecting between three and five percent of children globally. More than 50 percent of these children continue with these symptoms into adulthood. No doubt, it is a disorder that isn't helped by the fact many children leave school to confine themselves to a room where they escape with video games, internet, and social contact via cell phones. This does nothing to enhance their relationship with the great outdoors.

According to a study by the Chesapeake Foundation, children

---

3. Ibid., p. 159.

spend about six hours a day in front of a television or computer and only four minutes in structured outdoor play. The same study revealed that increasing the study of science and Nature in children proved beneficial in many areas, including improvement in cognitive functioning, reduction in symptoms of attention deficit disorder, and an increase in self-discipline and emotional well-being. Staring at smart phones and typing "LOL" at the end of every cryptic message hardly balances the mind, body, and spirit with our surroundings. While children these days exhibit incredible computer skills, how will these help once the electricity goes out for a while?

Most athletic programs in schools allow children to exercise their bodies and even their minds, but they cannot duplicate the relationship we are meant to have with Nature. Nature opens us up even more, especially when we are younger. Athletics is usually only an hour or two each day and most children do not pursue sports after high school, but Nature is always a part of our lives.

Nature Explore, the education program mentioned earlier based in Lincoln, Nebraska, focuses on educating children of all age groups, from infants to elementary-school-aged children. They also have pilot programs geared toward middle school and high school students. Tina Reeble at Nature Explore says that more than a decade's worth of research has shown that children tend to excel in an outdoor learning environment where they can express themselves in multiple ways simultaneously.

"So often in schools, learning has become about meeting standards and outcomes. We think we're educating more effectively by compartmentalizing learning. You go to math class and you learn math. You go to language arts and you learn how to spell. You go to physical ed and you move your body. But that's not how we work as human beings. As human beings it's everything all together all at the same time," says Reeble. "When we have opportunities to grow and learn in outdoor classrooms, that's often more engaging, more exciting for us as human beings because we're using our whole selves as learners. So it's the physical development, it's the cognizant development, and it's special emotional development—all taking place at the same time."

Programs like Nature Explore utilize design and designing principles in different areas to help children develop the proper learning skills. When children go to certain spaces, they know what activities to expect, for example, art, building, gardening, big body movement, and sand/dirt digging. The children are guided in those respective activities but make their own decisions about how to work.

"We know and understand the connection to Nature. However, from an educator point of view we truly consider the outdoors as a learning environment," says Reeble. "Just as we would carefully think of our indoor environment—making sure it's meeting the needs of every child in the ways that they learn but also what we want them to learn—we can do the same thing in the outdoor environment. We have different areas that help us make sure that children find themselves and rise to their best selves in the site because it accommodates every learning style, and there is a wide range of expanses and activity that can take place in there."

Nature Explore also offers a book and DVD entitled *Learning with Nature* that helps translate the message of an effective outdoor learning environment.

"We at Nature Explore don't have a curriculum because we don't believe there's one way to do this. We believe Nature provides unending possibilities of learning," Reeble says. "Anybody can find themselves no matter what your standards are. A huge message we want to get across is that this is an ideal venue to make learning exciting and meaningful for children."

Valle's dream is that all children be educated in some form of an outdoor environment in public schools. She maintains that many of the problems experienced by children relate to our complete disconnect from Nature. Programs like Urban Roots help tear down the wall between people and the great outdoors.

"All of the problems that we see in youth today, like ADD and such, I believe stem from the lack of kids being outdoors, learning about their nature through Nature. We all need to eat, period, and not educating youth about this is a disservice to humanity. Children are our most precious resource, our seeds. Just like the seeds we plant in the ground, they need to be nurtured and tended—and the more we do that, the more they thrive. When you stick a plant inside a florescent-lit room all day and expect it to grow, it won't. Why do we do this to our children?" asks Valle, who has a child of her own. "Giving children the opportunity to watch food grow and then learn how good it is to eat is one of the most critical things we can do as a society. Without it, as a society we are withering and dying. It is not too late, though, we can change this and we must. We must give our children the chance to get outside and grow."

Rather than taking one approach to education, making carbon copies of it across the country, and then institutionalizing it and forcing it upon our children as education through some sort of mandate or law, we need to encourage the creativity and imagination of each child. It's the same as working with any living creature—we cannot impose our will upon others and expect amazing results. Certain parts of the individual shut down when forced to perform like a mindless machine. Nature Explore places an emphasis on children being free to express themselves in their own unique ways. For example, their program sets aside time during which young children can move about freely and make their own choices.

"Their own ideas are generating their learning, which makes it more significant because the thought process is generating within themselves," says Reeble. "In more elementary- and middle-school age groups, we have teachers focusing more on taking [their] class to a specific area with a specific lesson in mind. They are using the outdoor space to help children deeply understand a particular concept. And it works because they're using their whole body, they're using their hands-on opportunity. So it's getting them out of the book and off the TV and getting it into their hands and minds firsthand."

Through the World Forum Foundation (www.worldforum foundation.org), parents and educators can learn more about these types of programs and how to incorporate these unique principles into public schools across the country. Nature Explore, Urban Roots, and many other programs exist to help educate not only families, but also schools in reaching children and adults.

"The message we're getting from college professors is that these students are coming in with a fear of Nature. Some parents come to us because they say they don't have the skills to teach their children, they don't know what to teach them when they are outdoors," says Reeble.

These programs exist to help reconnect children with Nature, so that when they are adults that relationship still exists, and they are able to pass it on to future generations. Computers, books, and television can entertain and educate us, but our real education is attained in the real world. Nature is as real as it gets.

"With young kids it's not a matter of helping them save the rain forests because cognitively, that's way more than they can handle," Reeble explains. "It's a matter of helping them learn to love the Earth, learn that the Earth, our environment, and human beings go together, so that when they are young adults they have that within their hearts and beings."

I Am Nature

I am Nature
Nature is me
taking walks
through my subconscious
through dreams
taking old man naps
beneath an old oak tree
I planted when just a boy

Wind howls my name
sun scorches my labor
autumn is a comforting transformation
as cold rattles mortal bones
reminding me of the fragility
the temporary nature of seasons
changing colors
evolving others
so we complete the cycle's circle
and wake
to find ourselves
dreaming the perfect dream

Take Me

Take me
not me
but someone who looks like me
tell them your story
change your mind
live someone else's life
then come back and tell me
what you think you might have seen
or heard
or thought
or felt

Even your dreams grow tired
if you ignore them long enough
the mind grows bored with impatience

Not every idea is genius
not every crime is wrong
but it is what comes of those ideas
how the failures succeed
how your conscious handles the crime
that is the story that becomes you

Self-Transgression

It's the transgressions
the tears and the fears
the things that go bump in the night
that move us, motivate us to points of some manifestation of self
of what was
what maybe should be
we lie there
sit there
staring into the heart of the nothingness
evident in every last set of eyes
present in all shouting voices of ill intent
and disguised in the true horror of bitterness
it's the true, sorrowful damnation in the art of forgetting
hoping somehow to rid ourselves
of that hallowed hole stuck in the middle of us all
some grand canyon spreading souls from wholes
dividing ourselves from others, ourselves from self
someday, maybe
there'll be some unexplainable eruption bringing back
        the continents of man
bringing back man to woman
humanity to Human Spirit
joining us all with not only ourselves
but with the eternal sense of love and faith and hope
linking us to the Great Spirit
to the concept of heaven
to every last angel's strumming hand on golden harps
        of harmony
I can see it all in fiery chariots blazing in tornadoes
I see bearded prophets prophesying

I see children crying of lost homes
I see parental worries soothed in the end of it all

and one day, our day, my friends, we'll all sit and laugh
      together
we'll sing and tell new stories
because nothing will be old
no tears or pain
no suffering or confusion
when all this nonsense is over and eternity
      is the golden thought
on every mind

Highway's Skull

Let's sail across these highways
piercing wind with sharpened skulls,
dancing across earth with rolling wheels
across mountain and valley
through laughter and pain
let us not lose heart or faith or momentum
though there are many miles to go,
the destination is in site
so climb aboard
buckle up
and smile
while the ride takes you home

Highway Signs

Bug stains
dirt road windshield
makes the sun seem like a dream
like the light at the end of a tunnel
you can see it
but you won't reach it
not now
not yet
running parallel
from everything

Sun bowing to Earth
slips golden coin in horizon's jukebox
to play night's tune
the hypnotic song of darkness

Shade of shadows
sky more gray
pure heavenly blue
giving way
moon shining
see man in moon
even though the moon
is all woman
vast shadows fade
no lights out here
small towns
headlights flicker

Signs boasting
Honda, Ford, Chevy

guns, booze, knives
rusted signs
old designs
rural architecture
pump jacks and barns
lonesome farm equipment
tired tractors and cotton strippers
big tank batteries
holding gas, butane, diesel
whatever petro fuels the future
and hides the ride's distraction
from personal recognition
avoiding the real signs of our existence
but small town progression is here
Hogg Welding machine
red brick car dealerships
farmer machine shops
meat-packing plant
goose-neck trailers
cottonseed
fast-food joints
slow-mind boutiques
convince us what to eat or wear

One lane
all traffic merge left
yes, all merge
always merging
get in line
one behind the other
slow the pace
ignore intuition
as the destination fades into amnesia

CHAPTER FOUR

Completing Our Circle
Being Who We're Meant to Be

It is not half so important to know as to feel.
RACHEL CARSON

Bare Feet Free the Mind

I am you. You are me.

With the passage of time, our minds and lives gain more clarity if we allow it. Tougher decisions are asked of us. But the decisions themselves aren't as difficult once we realize the path we are intended to walk and the life we are meant to live. The world we've allowed to be created often makes no sense. At one time or another, we've all felt this way. When conscious of supporting systems and ideas that are out of touch with our own personal beliefs, we choose to either bite our lip and continue to join the insanity or to get the hell out of Dodge and jump ship. Some of us build our own boats, setting sail for unfamiliar shores. We even take comfort in that unfamiliarity, just knowing that we've freed ourselves from false expectations of who we are and that we are beginning a journey into who we are meant to be.

For many years, we've known that we humans utilize less than ten percent of our brain. Yet, we're so confident in our mode of thinking, so quick to affirm the legitimacy of our own opinions, ideas, and feelings. We're so limited in our thinking process, yet we are unwilling to admit that to ourselves because of our self-imposed sanctions and boundaries. We censor our own thoughts with the restraints of linear thinking and "normal" expectations. Where do these limitations come from? What is the source of our failure to grasp so much more? Part of it is because of outside influence or peer pressure, part is merely due to self-denial. Most of it is because we are willingly plugged into a system designed to fail. It is up to us as individuals to disconnect from the monstrosity of this accepted method of living. Through our reconnection to Nature, those bridles, reigns, and other constraints fall to the side. The freeing of thoughts that comes with this allows us to gain a more accurate perspective of what life is or can be.

As children, we're taught to follow our dreams, be anything we want to be, and do anything we want to do. Our imaginations set us free in our youth. As we get deeper into adolescence and adulthood, our imaginations are smothered by an onslaught of rules and regulations designed to stuff us in a box and force us to make certain choices. Our options are usually yes or no, green or red, left or right. The concept of free will disguised as the illusion of here or there. Before we know it, our imaginations are nothing more than distant memories, and our minds are trained to accept a certain sequence of expectations.

I no longer allow myself to think in linear terms all of the time. Too often, I expected to take the next step on the staircase or climb the next rung on the ladder once I had achieved something greater than before. Often, I was greatly disappointed. Fooled by expectations in relation to time and progression, my ego would predict the next advancement by a certain date. This only led to frustration and confusion. Now, my mind often drifts into another world. This escape allows me to look at all possibilities, different outcomes, more rhymes and reasons than just the normal expectations we've been taught to adopt.

There are different gadgets in this modern world that help "ground" us to the Earth. They plug into an electrical outlet. Why are these even considered necessary? Because of humanity's genuine disconnection from Nature? Simply walking barefoot in the grass or open field for a few minutes every day will do the same thing these gadgets do. But are we grounded? Truly grounded? Are we connected to what's real? Or are we plugged into something false, something that is stealing the real us, sucking dry the essence of what the human species is supposed to be? We are intended to be the collective consciousness of this planet. It is time we began acting like we are worthy of this.

Some people have not only acted in accordance with the collective consciousness of the planet, they have lived it for a long time. Kay Shinol is a member of a group that calls themselves the "Awakening Tribe." Although they insist this involves everyone on the planet, the core group includes 50 people. Since 1990, the group has gathered together to reconnect to certain spiritual aspects through Nature. They've traveled to key geographical areas like Machu Picchu to "awaken one of the chambers of the heart of Earth Mother" and Denali National Forest in Alaska to "awaken the backbone of Earth Mother." Each year the group embarks on another adventure to a special sacred place, performing ceremonies to help reconnect Nature and humanity. Why?

Shinol says, "The message we keep getting is, 'Because we are the ones who put the wise ones to sleep!' It feels as if human beings separated from their truth and put the energy grid/network and the wise ones to sleep while they (humans) went down a different path. I can remember the Hopi Prophecy Rock, and it makes perfect sense in terms of the work we have been asked to do all these years."

Shinol has spent time with leaders of various native cultures across the world. In 1995, Peruvian Shamans visited Shinol's home in Austin, Texas. She says their visit was quite an adventure in itself.

"They told us that they had left their mountains and jungles because Great Spirit told them they needed to go into the world, find other native tribes, and share their ways. They were further told that it is time to put away your differences and teach Little Brother (Western humans) to get back to what I took to mean the Balance of Nature. While they were here I had the privilege of seeing this coming together of diverse tribal ways," says Shinol. "There were these Aborigines visiting the University of Texas, and I asked the Peruvians if they would like to go to the Aborigines' press conference at the capitol. So, they put on their colorful ceremonial clothes and crowded into my Honda.

"We parked and made our way to the capitol steps where banks of microphones stood waiting for the translator to put into English their message," she remembers. "Before I could say words of caution, the Peruvians walked through the crowds and up to the Aborigines. As the Peruvians knelt down, the Aborigines pulled them up and the whole thing became a hug fest. They were talking but neither side spoke the language of the other, and the UT translators were visibly frustrated. Finally, the University officials just let the two groups of native people go off to a nearby grassy area. They all sat down, grabbed hands, were laughing as if they had just met up with long-lost relatives. It was so beautiful to watch! I was told later that the Australians had also expressed the idea that they were told to go into the world and meet up with other tribes and teach Little Brother before it is too late . . . It's comforting to know that these tribal people living in Nature would leave their homes to tell us we must change our ways."

Shinol says the Awakening Tribe does not claim to fully understand the enormity or depth of their work, but she says it is work that is needed.

"It seems like for a long time, people have been 'out of touch' or disconnected from their origins, their stories, their ways," says Shinol. "While we may not understand the why of our work, we all feel it is a part of a movement that started some time ago . . . a movement to offer awareness of the huge blessings Nature has for us when we live in balance and harmony . . . and an awakening to the diversity in ways for living that way."

Over the years, I've witnessed this movement in small circles across the planet. But it is becoming ever more important that more of those circles overlap one another.

Unifying Our Communities

Leaving Texas on a winged machine in November of 2010, it was nice to get away from the barren dustiness of cotton fields being stripped to the bone. As I searched the faces of strangers in the melancholic halls of international airports, an overwhelming sense of fear bubbled to the surface of a seething pot of nervous anxieties. Where the hell were we all going? How soon would we get there? What would we be forced to reveal, hand over, explain, or have taken away before we reached our destination?

In the clouds was a sense of peace . . . perhaps nothing morbid could touch us there, some 40,000 feet from the Earth's surface. Distant lights twinkled below like stars from another galaxy. We were like ancient spirits hovering over it all, drinking in the mapped grid of a lost species' existence. Just when it seemed we were so far from anything else, we passed directly over several chemtrails crisscrossing the evening sky. Anxious thoughts invaded my mind once again.

Easing out of the clouds, gravity brought us back down to reality's level. I'd never seen New York City from the air at night. Spectacular. Tall buildings exploded from the darkness like roman candles. Billions of lights lit up the Earth like scattered neon marbles across a pitch-black room. Skyscrapers, bridges, city streets, apartment buildings, and all of urbanity's insanity smiled a twinkling smile. There was Manhattan. There was Liberty Island. I could see the base of the statue, but I couldn't see Lady Liberty. Where was the robe? Where was the tablet? Where was the torch? Had someone forgotten to change the light bulb? How many nights had she been in the darkness? Perhaps she was "closed for security purposes"? How fitting, I thought. Lady Liberty's torch had been snuffed long ago for our own security. The bastards didn't even bother keeping up the illusion of illumination anymore.

My journey through New York and New Jersey was one I'll never forget. I was greeted and welcomed by a wonderful soul who immediately felt like a long lost friend. And in those few days, I realized how powerful our connection with others can be. She is a fellow liberator herself and is much aware of this transition. Our conversations were not restricted by fear or political correctness. Just raw honesty about all of life. Even as we talked of noticeable signs of the failure of the infrastructure of once-proud neighborhoods that now resembled graveyards, we took faith in our awareness of where it was all going. We were so alive, even as so much seemed to be crumbling, quaking, or trembling around us. I cannot be thankful enough for what her spirit of companionship will always mean to my own personal existence.

Walking through the maze of hustle and bustle in Manhattan, she laughed, "Can you imagine a world where shopping was not our basis of existence?" I smiled because I could. We imagined what the streets would be like without all the gas-guzzling cars and taxicabs, if all the shouting and horn honking were replaced with music, laughter . . . and smiling people simply enjoying the gift of freedom. It was yet another epiphany daring to navigate its way through the hazy fog of modernization's confusion.

Walking down a single block I was able to hear a dozen different accents and another dozen languages. It was musical. People from all over the world brought together by the hope of a better life, guided to the United States by the glowing light of Lady Liberty's torch held high.

I was encouraged, even inspired, by the people of Brooklyn, where it appears many are determined to focus on the essentials of life and living. There was an energy there that I think can be contagious for the entire country. Beautiful art giving life to brick buildings. Rooftop gardens popping up like spring lilies. Intelligent conversations and ideas bringing people together to centralize communities around healthy, local food. Yes, now we were getting somewhere. Finally, an awakening I was so proud to see and be a part of—even if it was 1,800 miles from my home.

Speaking in a room full of enlightened souls, my heart and mind basked in the energy pulsing there. People were getting back to what fills the spirit and balances our minds and bodies with our hearts, getting back in touch with Nature despite the restrictions of urbanity.

Sitting at the head of the table for a panel discussion, I felt like the leader of my own tribe coming together with leaders of distant tribes. We wanted the same thing—peace, unity, strength through independence, and liberty through valiant actions. We wanted to stop fearing the unknown and embrace the beauty that comes through truly getting back to the fundamentals of life—(clean) water, (healthy) food, (affordable) shelter, and love in its unbridled form.

For many days after that I was glowing. Hope had found me. Our movement had begun. Our purpose confirmed in the illumination of Lady Liberty's blaze. The torch has been passed to us, my friends. We are the ones we've been waiting for all along.

Lessons of Consequence

We've sacrificed spirit for religion, poetry for advertising jingles, health for money, happiness for social acceptance, contentment for greed, liberty for security, and freedom for fear. Why? Is this what our parents taught us and their parents taught them? Or has it simply been methodically stomped into us through fear-driven tactics?

Fear is screamed from the overwhelming majority of headlines and newscasts. When we're not being convinced to be afraid, we're being convinced to buy something we don't really need. We're being programmed to accept ridiculous methods by which to exist while we lose extremely vital portions of ourselves that help cultivate higher vibrations of our true being. This is the society that has developed around us. This is the society we've allowed to be created. Moving forward, it us up to us what type of society we choose to participate in.

Music, theater, and art programs are being severed from the school curriculum throughout U.S. schools due to budget cuts, and more focus is being placed instead on reading, science, and math skills. We're not allowing our children to fully develop their artistic skills and creative minds, turning them more into robotic wage-earners rather than flesh-and-bone spirits with a voice. Nationwide, music programs have been reduced more than 50 percent in the past seven years. Music and other artistic expressions are our connection not only to Nature, but also to our own spirits within. They act as a voice, a note, a beat, a chord of resonance opening up something inside of us that is connecting elsewhere. Music is powerful. Often, I think we fear that power within ourselves, misinterpreting it as outside influence rather than inside guidance.

Deep down, I think we still fear Nature. Manifest Destiny and its ultimate pursuit of vast riches aided in conquering our fear temporarily. On the whole, we tend to fear what we can't control. And what scares the ever-living hell out of us is that we can't control Mother Nature. But from the stories of others within this book, we can see how incredible life can be when our connection with Nature is recognized and embraced. Rather than seeking little blue pills to cure our ills, we need to seek more of self, more of Nature, more of love in its many forms to help fulfill the purpose of our existence.

As our species has grown to vast numbers, frequently one culture has ended up invading another's land, forcing the inhabitants into slavery while coercing them into abandoning their spiritual beliefs, traditions, and culture altogether. Once the white man or European set foot here in the New World, he was hell bent on conquering not only the land, but also its inhabitants in search of valuable resources such as gold and silver and, later on, coal and oil. Our connection to the land and to wilderness became deeply rooted in fear and greed, not a reverence for Nature or ourselves.

Tracing numerous cultures of peaceful people throughout history, invariably a more technologically advanced and numerous people overtake them. Most of these hostile takeovers have been about resources in the form of land, gold, silver, coal, oil, timber, water, and so on. They seldom, if ever, have anything to do with religious or spiritual beliefs, although, once new territory is seized, the ruling empire forces its own belief system on the native people. Ruling others belittles the reasons for our existence.

Whether Persian, Babylonian, Egyptian, Greek, Roman, Chinese, Nordic, Moorish, British, Spanish, French, or American, empires have all exemplified greed, gluttony, and arrogance. In the construction of these empires, we've attempted to destroy the essence of the Human Spirit. How many millions of people have suffered at the hands of these empires so a few might prosper from the associated discoveries, takeovers, and advancements?

Still, to this day, we are prey to such a process. Historically, it has only occurred by one culture enslaving another culture: Egyptians enslaving the Jews; Australians enslaving Aborigines; Great Britain imprisoning India; America enslaving Indians, Africans, and Mexicans. Now that we've run out of foreign cultures to enslave, we enslave each other by submitting to a corrupt and rigged system.

While many governments do more to profit from their citizens than to protect them, corporations and elite families have piggybacked on these governments to gain an upper hand in modern civilization, turning people into nothing more than profit-churning peasants. Convinced to abandon a utopian world of expression through Nature, we plunge headfirst into a stockyard mentality and become lifelong voluntary coin collectors for the granddaddy piggy bank of them all. This, we are convinced, is the fulfillment of an existence so miraculous and mysterious that we dare not question the legitimacy of the scheme that brings it about.

Fleeting manipulative strategies of wealthy rulers are tearing us apart, inside and out. We are allowing a very small percentage of our species to rip out our spirits as they coax us to continue to decimate the Earth, all her beauty and her creatures simply so we can deliver more riches to these wealthy rulers and pocket very little for ourselves. They strip the Earth bare, using our own blood and bones as fertilizer to grow more money and power. They use our sweat and tears to water their diseased crops, poisoning the Earth and the Human Spirit. This is a game that has carried on for far too long. It is a process we have the power to stop . . . now. Not later. Right now. All we need is the will, the strength, the desire, and the ability to unite as one.

For years, the Hopi warned we were living in the eleventh hour. Now, they say we are in that final hour. Does that mean the end of everything for everyone? Hardly. It is simply the end of so many things we've grown accustomed to.

The common traits of this modern society we've created suppress who we really are, resulting in spiritual fatigue. The gears of our inner being are not aligned properly. It is our duty to realign these internal gears. Now is the time for us to wake up and take back our lives, take back our selves, take back our true purpose as flesh-and-bone spiritual beings living, breathing, walking, and talking in the most beautiful place we could have ever imagined.

These days are here for us to listen to the voice within. Our higher consciousness needs, wants . . . even demands our utmost attention to what is happening to us and Mother Earth.

A transition is occurring right now—one that is meant to welcome all things into our lives that will purify our true beings. Those who resist this cleansing will not make it through to the other side. Those who hear the voice of Nature will survive and begin to follow a path of balance, of harmony, and of great fulfillment, regaining an appreciation of what has been here on this Earth all along. It is a place of great peace and prosperity, but not the prosperity in terms of financial gain that we have grown accustomed to. This is one of enlightenment.

When life gets increasingly difficult, it is important we simplify living as much as possible. How do we perform such an about-face? By focusing on the essentials of living: water, food, shelter, and love. Sounds too easy for many of us. Perhaps it comes across as cheesy or too idealistic. But it is an effective remedy. Whenever an athlete or sports team is struggling, you will always hear that individual or team leader say, "We have to get back to the fundamentals of the game." In football, it is elements such as blocking and tackling. In baseball, fielding and hitting. Golf deals with the mechanics of the player's swing. In life, we must simply focus on the essentials that enable us to survive and thrive, namely, the water we drink, the food we eat, the house in which we dwell, and the people/environment we surround ourselves with.

Through the powerful persuasions of corporate advertising, religious beliefs, and societal peer pressure, we have been too easily convinced that the basics of living are anything but our connection to Nature and that part of our self that is in tune with all things. As many continue to cling to ideology that is meaningless, we will find life increasingly painful to the point of emotional paralysis. Clinging to the shore prevents us from going where we are intended. Letting go allows us to follow the river's flow.

Much of life is an illusion—simply a sideshow to distract us from our true being or higher consciousness. Our minds are manipulated to help create a world focused on fears, phobias, and other pessimistic emotions. This throws us off balance and out of touch with the mystical vibrations of life.

As Manifest Destiny inspired the growth of America, we were so focused on our own selfish desires for a newfound life that we thought nothing of the destruction of the people already here. This land was their home, and they understood the importance of Nature, of respecting all things, of taking only what was needed to survive and giving back as much or more. The balanced relationship Native Americans had with the Earth was a lesson we refused to learn and a concept we failed to live by. The further west we pushed, the more lives and livelihoods we destroyed. When we ran out of land, we built as fast and furious as possible, raiding the country's gold, silver, copper, and coal. Not satisfied with its metals and minerals, we then turned on Nature. We decimated the forests and the buffalo in exchange for paper money and temporary possessions. We waged war on peaceful people. We raped and pillaged, yet labeled these people savages. We were the savages. We destroyed their way of living, convincing them they needed to change for the better, forcing them to abandon their own language, spiritual beliefs, and cultural practices. Considering ourselves superior, we arrogantly ridiculed their harmonic existence as primitive naivety.

Centuries later, our disturbing trends continue. With a dire expansion in the number of inhabitants armed with heavy machinery and fossil fuel to drive it, our destruction is more grave than ever. We destroy mountaintops to satisfy our demand for coal. We drain water reservoirs to quench our undying thirst. We dam rivers to supply electricity for overpopulated metropolitan communities. We plow under the prairies to feed our bellies. We destroy pristine wilderness for modern expansion. We remove Nature's gifts to entertain ourselves with consumerism and numerous decoys.

These trends must end before we destroy more than we are capable of restoring in a generation. Unless we are out to end our own existence or at least that of the vast majority, we must change and begin to emulate Nature—not manipulate her. We must seek balance, not supremacy. Each day we wake with vigor and undertake this change is our finest hour. Each moment we spend preparing for it is our greatest truth. Each bead of sweat we shed in our efforts toward a better planet is an affirmation of our glorious existence and our significance in the universe.

So here we are, smack dab in the heart of 2012. So many predictions, so little time. If you're reading this, the world hasn't ended, so perhaps we can get on with our much overdue transition. Perhaps we're at long last getting closer to admitting that, although time is relevant, it is our own actions and reactions that are the real trigger point, not some manifested collection of predictions of doomsday by a specific date.

Whether or not you've read the book of Revelations is not the point. Let's not waste all our energy focusing on the hype of an apocalyptic prediction . . . whichever religion's version it may be. Our minds, our thinking patterns have the power to influence our lives in one direction of another. What we think, we create. The mind is extremely powerful and influential if you have billions focused on the same thought. We are the ones who help evolve this planet. Where are our minds now? What have our thought patterns been the past few years? Do we believe exactly what we hear on the news? Or do we draw our own conclusions by balancing our hearts, minds, and spirits?

We are far too busy surrendering to the written laws of man in his corrupt corporate portrayal of existence to truly embrace a marriage or reconnection of Nature and the Human Spirit. To recover, we must revolt against this system designed to override our natural instincts. No revolution, whether internal or external, will succeed without us empowering our own selves with knowledge and action. But whatever war is waged externally to overthrow old systems, the final battle will be won internally. Let us not continue to buy into a series of misconceived notions. Let us define our own version of normality by blazing our own trail.

When one arrives at the point of accepting just how screwed up the world really is, there is a decision to be made. What do you do with this realization? After all, intelligence without action is as worthless as a steering wheel on a bull. You have to ask yourself some serious questions. Do you say, "Screw it, there's nothing I can do to change it"? Or do you get up off your ass and start changing your life for the better? Do you begin to be that change you want to see in the world? Do you encourage others to do the same, even if it is uncomfortable to bring up in conversation? Do you dare risk social acceptance or legitimacy among your peers? Do you dare draw attention to yourself by being the one in the crowd who stands up in defiance?

We must each be the one who throws open the window and screams, "I'm mad as hell, and I'm not going to take it anymore!" And once we close that window and return to our lives, we need to channel that rage into action.

We cannot accept fake food. We cannot accept contaminated oceans and rivers. We cannot accept poisoned soil. We cannot accept poisoned water. We cannot accept poisoned bodies. We cannot accept the extinction of more species or the slow, methodic annihilation of our own kind. We cannot accept "unexplained" die-offs any longer. We cannot accept systems that are not sustainable. We cannot accept corporate control. We cannot accept government ineptitude. We cannot accept the lies another single day.

We will never be at peace with ourselves until we are at peace with Nature. Our bond is sacred. Our personal relationship with Nature is as important as our relationship with any family member or friend. Sitting idly in the shadows as the madness continues will not change anything or bring about what we know needs to happen.

We must be that change that we know needs to occur. And not years from now . . . but right now. Time is not on our side. Conveniently ignoring this vital information simply because the majority is will not make any of this horror go away. In fact, it will only make it get worse at a much faster pace.

There is a message for those of us living now. Hope. Hope for all. Not the kind of hope marketed and sold in political campaigns or the kind used to pimp the latest, greatest product. Real hope. The kind of hope that inspires, strengthens, and brings love. Does life end with a whimper or a cry? Does it end with us fighting one another? Fighting over dwindling resources, power, money, land, religious differences, fears, philosophies, misconceptions of freedom, or just plain survival? Or does it end the same way it began—hearts beating in unison to a sacred drum?

Our Way-Overdue Epiphany

Perhaps it's too painful to admit we've built a machine far too large and far too destructive. After all, we've been working tirelessly toward these underlying concepts of expansion, progression, and perpetual growth for centuries. For us to be the ones to witness the resulting high-speed chase of mass extinction, confessing we've had a hand in it on one level or another, is a rather daunting and sobering admission. The answer does not lie in chopping up the larger machine to make smaller carbon copies. The answer is a different model.

The greed that grips the guts of this country and this planet is vile. Its claws are sharpened on our fears. This is old greed, ancient greed, passed on from one generation to another. It is fostered, nurtured, and encouraged by the highest of places that rule our economic systems, government, and minds using techniques of social suppression and spiritual deflation. Who knows how long it's really been around? As long as love? Unlikely. But probably not long after love came along, greed peered out from the shadows then slowly, methodically made its way to center stage, convincing love it needed a rest. And while love rested, greed prolonged the sleep into a coma with one steady dose of pills and potions after another. Love woke only occasionally to use the bathroom or get a drink or find out what the weather was like before smiling, yawning, scratching its ass, and going back to bed.

This ancient greed has crept into the hearts of many. It does not reside solely in government capitols and Wall Street. Greed runs and ruins the lives of many. Whether it is a farmer who spends his or her entire life trying to squeeze out as much money from the earth as possible, or a real estate tycoon who chews up and spits out an entire community of people to build a mega shopping mall and parking lot, or a logging company that destroys acres of ancient trees in our national forests—greed is all around us.

We can blame this greed on corporations. We can blame this greed on government. But it is human. It is real. And it's tearing us apart. So how then do we rid ourselves of this disease? By waking love from its coma and making damned sure it doesn't fall back to sleep. We purge ourselves of greed, replace it with a desire for balance and unity, a passion for restoration and healing, as well as the strength to overcome the pain of being reborn. No longer should survival be viewed as "kill or be killed" but rather "heal and be healed."

For many years, humanity has suffered through one hell of an identity crisis. Why? Because we've chosen to live separate from everything else and consider ourselves far superior to any and all living creatures. We share this philosophy and have divided ourselves from other countries, other races of people, acting as if imaginary borders and skin pigmentation were true bases for division. Whether it is someone who belongs to another religion, speaks another language, or dresses significantly different than our own group, we feel that alienating them in our minds is the best way to verify the value of our own personal choices and beliefs. If we have general disdain for others of our own species, how then can we ever expect to experience genuine peace and unity with all living creatures?

What we think, we create. What we do will leave a lasting imprint of who we were and what our intentions were focused upon during our lives. Everything is connected: our thoughts to our actions, our actions to our intentions, our intentions to our reason for living, for wanting to live. What is our legacy now? What remnants of our selves have we left behind for others to build upon?

Is spirit concerned only with Human Spirit? Or is spirit concerned with the spirit of all? Spirit, whether in human or animal or tree or rock or river or wind is still spirit. This connecting of the dots allows us to not only see but feel everything here. It provides an unveiling of emotion, a grand recognition of the transformation needed within all of us.

Fear is the antithesis of spiritual growth. It prevents us from being who we are meant to be. Fear is the one thing that keeps us out of balance. Our fight-or-flight instinct to numerous threats continually throws us off center. Our thoughts readily focus on negative outcomes rather than positive ones. Mental energy feeds unhealthy patterns, which create unhealthy living and an unhealthy world. We can no longer feed this fear machine. We can no longer fall for this ruse.

One thing we fear more than the boogeyman is inconvenience. Over the past 70 years, we've grown accustomed to everything being so convenient and cheap. It's time to refocus our energies and priorities . . . even if it is inconvenient to our current lifestyles. Eventually it will lead to a simpler life with more leisure time—one in which inconvenience is no longer an issue. Do not cower in bunkers and shelters, fearing the end. Live. Be free. Expect a new beginning. Anticipate greatness. Imagine a place, a world that allows us to express who we truly are.

We stopped listening to the voices of our minds, hearts, and souls and started listening to the voices coming out of radios and television sets as if they were beacons emitting heavenly light with messages from our version of God or a Higher Power. We were so fascinated by these contrivances, by the opportunities they offered to make life easier, more comfortable, more "advanced," that we failed to realize what they were doing to our true selves. So we began feeding our egos and slowly yet surely lulled our higher consciousness to sleep.

Fashion trends and many other pop culture influences override most aspects of our higher self. As we entered the 21st century, we reached more than just a landmark anniversary. We started entering another paradigm. Some will use this word to describe it, others may use another. The name given to this time period is not important, only our actions and reactions during it are. But for our own entertainment's sake, let us call it the Age of Reawakening. Many of us have felt this reawakening inside for many years, some are just beginning to recognize it. Children now are born with the ability to reawaken. So were we, but it is much stronger now. Today's children will be the warriors, healers, and teachers. They are the ones who will already know what is written or discussed in this book.

In order for us to survive the transition ahead, our egos must surrender to our higher consciousness. Again, let's not get caught up with word selection. Instead of "higher consciousness," many have called it God, Jesus, Buddha, Allah, Muhammad, or Spirit; others have tagged it Energy, Flow, Universe, Consciousness, or some other form of "higher power." It is simply that part of us that has always existed, that has always been inside us but has not been allowed to be the focal point because of the brain-staining caused by a barrage of distractions.

As we leave the cocoon of our former selves behind, we must not fear what we will become. Form yourselves into the image of something else. Not someone else, something else, whether it be the wind, the rain, a tree, your favorite pet, a river, a honeybee, a forest, an ocean, a dolphin, or a rock. It is important we begin seeing, feeling, and thinking about life in a very different way—a way that will not only fulfill us on many levels, but will also tell us the true story of who we are, where we are, and why.

Perhaps it is difficult for us to imagine replacing a way of life we were taught was a dream come true, an honor, a privilege. But ask yourself what it is that you would want to inherit. What do you wish to pass on to your children and future generations? Is it really money, power, convenience . . . or fear? What is to be done with this money and power? Usually, they are used to obtain more of the same. What is to be done with more convenience? Usually, it just creates expectations of even greater convenience. And fear? Fear is a cancer that consumes our existence. It spreads to destroy the whole.

On the other hand, it is easy to say, "I want world peace and I want to end hunger." Really? What are you doing about that? Simply stating or thinking I want this or that does not make it happen. Start by securing peace and healthy food for you, your family, and your community. Do that first and let it be contagious.

Another one of my favorite expressions is, "God will take care of us." Why would She/He do that? Are you the chosen one? How many good people have died prematurely or suffered greatly? Saying something and doing nothing gets us nowhere. Just as seeds need rain, words need action so that they may produce the needed outcome.

The only ones who can take care of us and what surrounds us are ourselves, our families, friends, neighbors, and most importantly, Mother Nature. As we look inside ourselves and begin this healing, we will help inspire others near us, and this healing will spread to our surrounding environment. Our heavily subsidized lifestyles are nearing their end. At the end of the day, we have only our own wisdom, our own skills, our own resources, and our own strengths to help us survive the transition to a more meaningful life.

May the words of this book be a part of our *Hanta ho*, our clearing the way. Today is a good day to die and be reborn. Every day is a rebirth . . . a second chance . . . another opportunity to recapture what was always intended. Today is a good day to let the voice of our spirit speak strong and clear through us so we may hear who we are supposed to be, what we are supposed to do, and where we should go. The path already exists. The only question is how many of us are willing to take the steps necessary for such a fateful journey? Our greatest challenge is surviving ourselves. Our obstacles in this pursuit involve overcoming misconceptions of reality that have been pounded into our minds, breaking free of greed and corruption's powerful persuasions, as well as persisting through the paralysis of fear. All the while, we plant new seeds that will continue to awaken and transpire life through peace, joy, strength, and love.

The clearing of our way is through Nature. It is only through Nature that we survive, that we exist. She is our Mother. If we open our hearts more than our minds, we will see that this is true. We must protect Her. We must save what is left of our forests, for the large trees are some of the greatest, oldest teachers on our planet. We must protect our oceans, for they breathe life into the entire world. We must protect our rivers, streams, and creeks, for they are the Earth's arteries and veins pulsing with life's blood. We must protect our mountaintops, for they give us a clearer perspective on the world. We must protect our soil, the earth itself. We must listen to Nature. We must learn to do this now.

There is so much energy, so much change, so much healing happening right now that it is difficult for our brains to keep up. I believe we have to check our egos at the toll booth and let our spirits get behind the wheel. Though weary, though confused, we must plunge onward . . . to fight the good fight, to find fragments of our true selves, to find old loved ones, to hear whatever language, learn whatever culture is needed to complete our true being.

Our view of Nature as either a commodity or a postcard image will slowly but surely fall away as we progress deeper into this century and deeper into the meaning of our true selves. Most of the suffering we've experienced will manifest something greater that strengthens our will and reinforces our hope of finding peace, happiness, and love. At some point, we will no longer look at life as suffering. Eventually, all of this emotion will melt into being. Somewhere down the line, we will recognize all of this as the only way the essence of who we really are could have been revealed.

We are in the early stages of worldwide revolution. As the Occupy Wall Street Movement has spread across the nation and the globe, transforming into Occupy Everything, it is evident the natives are restless. The peasants don't want to just "eat cake." We want a different reality. We seek another path. We want love to wake up and kick greed's ass to the curb. We want our lives to be more than an economic contribution to "elite" corruption and greed. We don't want the bullshit concepts of liberty and freedom marketed through television advertising for convertibles, cell phones, and designer jeans. We don't want shallow victories in meaningless wars against innocent countries. We want to live with true freedom, liberty, and love. This is more than a social and civil revolution. This is an existence revolution. We are the power of the storm.

The message for us is clear—we must revolt, change, evolve, transform, shift, and transcend in order to survive. We must transform one way of living into another. Form one way of thinking into another. Exchange our current set of expectations for another. This is achieved through thinking and doing, through innovating and creating. We are creators, not destroyers. We are living beings, the collective consciousness of this incredible planet. We are mind and body, but we are also imagination and spirit. We are the change. We are the path. We are the feet that will lead the way. We are the message and the voice to speak its truths.

This is a revolution for all to join. This is a battle for life, for a better path, for a new paradigm that frees us from our self-imposed sentence. We have the power to change ourselves and this world for the better. Knowledge is power, but just knowing isn't enough. Continuous action and reaction are also needed to complete our empowerment. We must empower ourselves in order to truly survive and thrive in this life. This empowerment will awaken everything within, connecting us to all things. This connection strengthens not only who we are, but more importantly, who we are meant to be. We are flesh and bone, but we are also spirit. We are Nature. We are the power of the storm, for we are the storm that has already passed and the one that is forming along the horizon's edge. We are one another. We are everything.

I Am You

I am you
you are me
side by side
a fulfillment of
our thoughts
our dreams
our fears
our regrets
our lessons learned
and our messages forgotten

It is difficult
to realize much
when we consider
ourselves separate,
it is difficult
to grasp the enormity
of our existence
if we consider
each other strangers

That Soul of Yours—Part I

'Tis that time when I not only ponder
where we all are in these cities and towns
and specks of the world we've scattered ourselves
but I'm sincerely curious what you are doing this morning
    in the universe
and how you are doing it
in terms of the soul
    in terms of a smile getting bigger
        in terms of a heart beating more fulfilled

And I think of a time, a place, some great significant event
when we shall all gather together
to laugh and cry
    jump and sing
        dance and shout
unifying some realness of spirit that pops and crackles
    in night's fire
blazing up into tiny flashes and sparks of burning yellows
    and orange

Flow in the efflux of vast and magical breezes
sending us to the four corners and back
to see lands of unseen proportion
    to hear cries of wind
        moans of sea
            laughter in sky
that we might sit back with hands behind dreaming
    heads and smirk
And with astonishment of this life we all live
the potentiality of harmony
    the beauty of friendship

the mystique of heart and soul
come all ye laborious poets
all ye messengers of today and yesterday and what
    tomorrow brings
ye heroes and villains
    ye bastards and priests
        ye magicians and prophets
            ye magistrates and guardians
                of the eternal prisms
all ye majestic men and all ye wonderful women
let us join together and kick free from the straps that bind
    and confine
and hide our souls from the rest of the world
let us push free from the shore
to gather momentum for the new journey

Hoist your sails!
smell the sea
kiss Heaven's starry dusks and colorful dawns
and feel the gift of wind
the magic of the water's path cutting and crossing
across forever to a new land
where lovers kiss
and friends smile
where there is no end or beginning
only the immeasurable feast of love
    of song
        of nothing but the pureness of spirit
           and the child in us all

peace
    love
        and the oneness of it

That Soul of Yours—Part II
(12 years later)

'Tis that time
when I realize once again
that there is no such thing as time
only man's attempt to measure
what we can't comprehend
due to our compulsive behavior
to feel like we have a handle
on everything
when in reality
we've lost our grip
on practically everything

I'm only curious of our choice
at the fork in the proverbial road
which road do we choose?
which way do we feel compelled to go?
out of obligation or spite
a path of least resistance
or a recovery of Nature and the Human Spirit?
that is the only choice

Our laughter cannot hide our tears
just as our songs cannot drown out
the greatest of our children's fears
we are not broken
only calloused
we're worn leather
not fine silk
weathered sailors
not greenhorns

The poets are all now rock stars
destroying motel rooms with boredom and insecurity
heroes and villains are disguised as the other
refusing to accept the vice of circumstance
the priests fallen from heaven's grace
due to centuries of sexual suppression and lies
the magicians turned to illusionists
whose tricks are exposed behind the fallen curtain
and prophets are too busy predicting
when this world will end and why

And time
yes, time
the very thing that brought us here together
well if it's real
it's still ticking
telling us the sails are torn
that we must row for distant shores
that our party has come to an end
and now our field of labor awaits
for us to heal
to right the wrong
to fix the problem
created by overindulgence
by ignoring the people we thought
were properly in place
to keep us on the floor
our dance is over
but our song has only begun to play
as we hoist instruments of choice
and take our place onstage

About the Author

A farmer, naturalist, and activist, Eric Herm was raised on a cotton farm near Ackerly, Texas. He left the farm to pursue other interests, traveling extensively in America, Mexico, Europe, and Northern Africa. The lifestyles and cultures he experienced and the people he met helped open his mind to the endless means by which to live a richer, more fulfilling life. Herm later returned to the land that has been in his family for nearly a century and re-dedicated his life to farming. His first book, *Son of a Farmer, Child of the Earth*, was published in 2010.

For more information, visit the author's website:
www.sonofafarmer.com

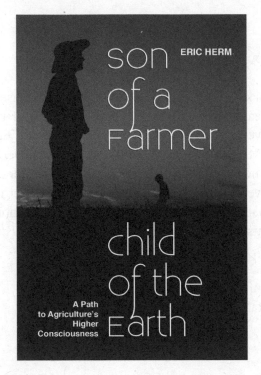

Also by Eric Herm

Son of a Farmer, Child of the Earth examines the strain of commercial agriculture's methods on our natural resources, ecosystems, and the farmer. As a fourth-generation farmer, Herm describes firsthand experiences with GMO crops, excessive chemicals, soil degradation, and other problems caused by an industry focused on quantity over quality. Combining personal observation and careful research, he offers clear solutions to each problem and provides ample resources for a healthier and more self-sufficient lifestyle. Herm's strong, direct message is not only for farmers, but humanity as a whole, to embrace our role as flesh-and-bone guardian angels of the Earth.

Recommended by the Organic Consumers Association.

SURVIVING OURSELVES